Praise for *Doing Both*

"*Doing Both* shows how Cisco turns business questions into market answers, offering real-life examples that will benefit forward-looking leaders."

—**Jeff Immelt**, Chairman and CEO, GE

"The best business books build around a single idea, often contrarian and counterintuitive. Everyone knows you can't have your cake and eat it, too. One of the first things you learn at business school is that management is about making difficult choices. Well, not always. This book persuades the reader that in decision making 'and' is often better than 'or.' Well worth the read."

—**Sir Terry Leahy**, CEO, Tesco

"Companies are often confronted with false choices, such as disruptive *or* sustaining innovation and optimization *or* reinvention. This book draws on Cisco's impressive track record over the last decade to illustrate that the correct strategy is always to do both."

—**Ratan Tata**, Chairman, Tata Group

"I have a very short personal list of 'most-admired companies,' and Cisco is one of them. Its management team has figured out how to break many 'either-or' tradeoffs that limit most companies' abilities to innovate and grow. This book is a lucid, cogent chronicle of how they do this. Your entire management team should read it."

—**Clayton Christensen**, Robert & Jane Cizik Professor of Business
Administration, Harvard Business School,
and author, *The Innovator's Dilemma*

"Insightful recommendations from a key executive within Cisco, the game-changing leader in networking for the Internet."

—**Garth Saloner**, Philip H. Knight Professor, and Dean,
Graduate School of Business, Stanford University

"*Doing Both* brings together many powerful lessons behind the story of Cisco, a company with a long record of delivering consistent innovation and strong business results. I encourage senior executives to embrace the challenges presented in this thoughtful book."

—**Dominic Barton**, Global Managing Director,
McKinsey & Company

"*Doing Both* simply amazed me. Sidhu, with graceful and clear writing, freshly imagines how successful enterprises—all enterprises—will not just survive but will flourish and prosper. Throwing away the trite and false dichotomies that too often paralyze and weaken organizations, this book, more than any other I've read in years, will be the most useful for this and future decades. This book is beyond a 'must-read.' It will be a necessity for all leaders to succeed in these tumultuous times."

—**Warren Bennis**, Distinguished Professor of Business,
University of Southern California, and author, *On Becoming a Leader*
and *Still Surprised: A Memoir of a Life in Leadership*

"In clear and graceful prose, Inder Sidhu provides practical lessons by describing the execution and innovation strategies that have made Cisco a worldwide leader. Definitely a book I would recommend."

—**Laura Tyson**, S.K. and Angela Chan Professor of Global Management, Haas School of Business, University of California-Berkeley, and Former Dean, London Business School and Haas School of Business

"Cisco is one of the world's most admired companies—and for good reason. Inder Sidhu reveals how Cisco drives profits and increases innovation, and provides readers with the pivotal insights that are necessary to do both."

—**Marc Benioff**, Chairman and CEO, salesforce.com

"A remarkable view of how one of the truly great companies of our time has consistently proven its ability to sustain and innovate, *Doing Both* is both an inspiring tale of triumph and a practical guidebook for leaders seeking answers to challenging questions about how to move their businesses forward in this new world. A must-read."

—**Ram Charan**, Business Advisor and best-selling author

"Great management is about transcending trade-offs, about 'turning either/or' into 'both/and.' In this timely and insightful book, Inder Sidhu takes you inside one of the world's most successful companies and shows you what it takes to be both disciplined *and* creative, highly optimized *and* perpetually inventive, tight *and* loose. This is a practical and valuable read for any leader who is eager to escape the limits of management-as-usual."

—**Gary Hamel**, Visiting Professor at London Business School, Director of the Management Lab, and author, *The Future of Management*

"Storytelling is central to all great firms, enabling the culture to carry forward its past and communicate its future. Cisco is no exception. It has wonderful tales to tell, and in Inder Sidhu we get a narrator who has the added advantage of having been an insider for much of the company's meteoric success. The result is both insightful and entertaining, and I encourage you to read this book."

—**Geoffrey Moore**, author, *Crossing the Chasm* and *Dealing with Darwin*

"On the one hand, great companies know where they want to add value a decade from now and the investment needed to get there. On the other hand, investors want proof that the management team can execute today. 'Doing both' means establishing investor credibility in the short term so long term goals can be pursued. Sidhu shows how Cisco is doing just that."

—**Gary Reiner**, CIO, GE

"*Doing Both* provides a simple and succinct set of strategies for the 21st century, using Cisco as an example of a company that has benefited from these strategies. With Sidhu's firsthand knowledge of Cisco, the explanations are logical and practical. A must-read for business leaders and management students."

—**Kris Gopalakrishnan**, CEO and Managing Director, Infosys Technologies

Doing Both

Doing Both

How Cisco Captures Today's Profit and
Drives Tomorrow's Growth

Inder Sidhu

Vice President, Publisher: Tim Moore
Associate Publisher and Director of Marketing: Amy Neidlinger
Executive Editor: Mary Beth Ray
Editorial Assistant: Pamela Boland
Development Editor: Russ Hall
Operations Manager: Gina Kanouse
Senior Marketing Manager: Julie Phifer
Publicity Manager: Laura Czaja
Assistant Marketing Manager: Megan Colvin
Cover Designer: Alan Clements
Managing Editor: Kristy Hart
Project Editor: Anne Goebel
Copy Editor: Language Logistics, LLC
Proofreader: Kathy Ruiz
Indexers: Ken Johnson, Lisa Stumpf
Senior Compositor: Gloria Schurick
Manufacturing Buyer: Dan Uhrig

Publishing as FT Press

Upper Saddle River, New Jersey 07458

FT Press offers excellent discounts on this book when ordered in quantity for bulk purchases or special sales. For more information, please contact U.S. Corporate and Government Sales, 1-800-382-3419, corpsales@pearsontechgroup.com. For sales outside the U.S., please contact International Sales at international@pearson.com.

Printed in the United States of America

First Printing June 2010

ISBN-10: 0-13-708364-5
ISBN-13: 978-0-13-708364-0

Pearson Education LTD.
Pearson Education Australia PTY, Limited
Pearson Education Singapore, Pte. Ltd.
Pearson Education North Asia, Ltd.
Pearson Education Canada, Ltd.
Pearson Educación de Mexico, S.A. de C.V.
Pearson Education—Japan
Pearson Education Malaysia, Pte. Ltd.

Library of Congress Cataloging-in-Publication Data

Sidhu, Inder
    Doing both : how Cisco captures today's profit and drives tomorrow's growth / Inder Sidhu.
        p. cm.
    ISBN-13: 978-0-13-708364-0 (hardcover : alk. paper)
    ISBN-10: 0-13-708364-5 (hardcover : alk. paper) 1. Cisco Systems, Inc. 2. Computer industry—United States—Management. I. Title.
    HD9696.2.U64C5764 2010
    338.7′62139810973—dc22
                        2010006414

To my wife, Deepna
You make all this possible.

and

To my Mother
You always believed in me.

Contents

Acknowledgments

When I first began work on this book at the end of 2008, the world was in a different place. The Dow Jones Industrial Average, for example, hovered around 9,000, but it would soon lose 2,500 points. Layoffs were in the headlines, and many executives were hunkered down.

Having worked through several recessions, I turned my thoughts to the future. In time, I knew, most business leaders would, too. When they did, I wanted to have something for them to read that could serve them in good times and in bad. To do that, I needed some encouragement and some assistance. For their encouragement, I want to thank John Chambers, Rick Justice, Rob Lloyd, and Ron Ricci.

For storytelling help, I turned to T.C. Doyle. T.C. gave life to my stories and brought a unique voice to the book. He deserves credit not only for his outstanding writing style, but also for many of the insightful stories that support the Cisco examples.

As editor and project manager, Sarah Halper was instrumental in shaping every chapter of the book. Sarah translated my vision into actionable plans and kept the book on track, revision after revision. Her dedication was unparalleled: Sarah worked tirelessly to move the project from start to finish, never missing a single deadline.

Of course, this project would never have been possible if Cisco's senior leaders had not been so generous with their time and insights. It was their depth of candor and quality of observations that helped inspire many of our stories. For this, I want to thank Tony Bates, Sue Bostrom, Surinder Brar, Gary Bridge, Frank Calderoni, Owen Chan, Blair Christie, Marthin de Beer, Carlos Dominguez, Wim Elfrink, Keith Goodwin, Stuart Hamilton, Kathy Hill, Ned Hooper, Laura Ipsen, Rebecca Jacoby, Soni Jiandani, Guido Jouret, T.S. Khurana,

Mario Mazzola, John McCool, Angel Mendez, Gary Moore, Paul Mountford, Edzard Overbeek, Pankaj Patel, Larry Payne, Edison Peres, Joe Pinto, Randy Pond, Blake Sallé, Dan Scheinman, Brian Schipper, Padmasree Warrior, and Tae Yoo.

Many Cisco colleagues also lent a hand so that we could bring you our story. For their willingness to reflect on their personal histories, dig up old emails and presentations, review countless chapters, and help align the messaging, allow me to thank Kash Abbasi, Barbara Adey, Graham Allan, Terry Anderson, Bruce Botto, Jonathan Cohen, Kathy Doyle, Lynn Easterling, Aimee Fuller, Ivan Gonzalez-Gallo, Laura Graves, Karla Lacey, Mick Lopez, Kathleen Makranyi, Ammar Maraqa, Vlada Marjanovic, Marilyn Mersereau, Alice Nagle, Quan Nguyen, Gareth Pettigrew, Michael Putz, Mike Rau, Rob Salvagno, Steve Sinclair, Marc Surplus, Mukundh Thirumalai, Erik Ullander-son, Naresh Wadhwa, Julianne Whitelaw, and especially Shailendra Gupta.

In addition to these colleagues, I want to thank my executive assistant, Heather Scharnow. Not only did she set up hundreds of appointments and manage multiple agenda items seamlessly, but she also fueled our energies with sugary treats whenever needed.

I would be remiss if I didn't offer my heartfelt gratitude to several people at Pearson Publishing. That includes Mary Beth Ray, Amy Neidlinger, Anne Goebel, Chrissy White, and the rest of the FT Press editorial, marketing, and production teams. And special thanks to publisher Tim Moore for telling us when our writing worked and when it made his hair hurt. A better team of publishing advisors, I could not ask for. I also want to acknowledge Danny Stern, Nicole Gagnon, Stephanie Heckman, Laura Moss, and the rest of the team at Stern + Associates for their contributions.

I want to thank my mother for always encouraging me and believing in me from day one. And my children Sonia, Sabrina, and Neal, for their patience and endless enthusiasm. Seeing them every day reminds me of all that is good in the world.

Lastly, and most importantly, I want to thank my wife, Deepna. Without her countless sacrifices, this book would not have been possible. Not only has she enabled my success every step of the way, she even found time to provide encouragement and insightful suggestions on the manuscript. I am so blessed to have her as my life partner.

Author's Note to the Reader

I don't think I have ever seen my mother look so beautiful—or be at such a loss for words.

But there she was, softly sobbing tears of joy 8,000 miles away. Despite the distance, I could see her as clearly as these words of text before your eyes. I remember the individual strands of her hair, the shimmer of her jewelry, and the bright color of her dress. Clearly, she had dressed up for the occasion—her first TelePresence call with her son in America.

My mother, of course, doesn't understand the video and communications technology that makes it possible for her to sit in a room in New Delhi, India, and see her grandchildren in San Jose, California. All she knows is that with the mere touch of a button, she can interact with her grandchildren in life-sized, living color. That, and the fact that I work for the company that makes it possible: Cisco.

Now 25 years old, Cisco is the world's largest maker of networking equipment—everything from the router in your home office to the massive systems that power the Internet. We also pioneered TelePresence, the video technology so easy to use that a teary-eyed grandmother can master it, yet so advanced that she can see the gleam in her seven-year-old grandson's eyes as he shows her his toys from a world away.

Today, Cisco is a global force in technology that generates annual sales approaching $40 billion and employs more than 60,000 employees. Hard to believe, but when I started in 1995, it had less than $2 billion in annual sales and 4,000 employees.

My oldest daughter was born soon after I joined the company. Over the years, I have shared in the ups and downs of my three children and the company alike as each has grown and matured. I held my daughter's hand as she took her first steps in California and helped Cisco as it made its first forays in China.

While my leadership positions have taken me around the world, they have also given me a unique perspective here at the company's headquarters. From my seat on Cisco's operating committee, for example, I participate in key decisions that contribute to Cisco's successes.

These internal decisions are rewarding, but the lessons I have learned from the ever-changing external environment are equally important. I was there for Cisco's meteoric rise when it became the most valuable company on the planet during the late-1990s boom years. I also experienced its catastrophic fall in the wake of the 2001 dot-com bust, when revenue dropped by nearly half in a single quarter. As part of the leadership team, I helped the company through its gradual recovery and return to prosperity.

Though excruciating, these experiences have served us well during the recent global recession. Cisco is weathering this storm better than most, due not only to the lessons learned nearly a decade earlier, but also to the pioneering management practices developed since then.

For all of this lore, many of the things that Cisco does to perpetuate its success are not widely practiced or even known outside the company. So I decided to share my perspectives in this book. Call it a story about practitioners, for practitioners, by a practitioner. Whether your company is emerging from a challenging time or growing faster than you ever imagined, I hope that you can benefit from my experiences.

Before I get to how Cisco captures today's profits and drives tomorrow's growth, allow me to tell you a little bit more about myself. I was born in India in the 1960s. The son of an army officer and a homemaker from a small town in Punjab, I came to America in the 1980s to continue my education after studying engineering in India. I earned an engineering degree from the University of Massachusetts. From there, I worked as an engineer, first at Intel, then at a small Silicon Valley start-up company through its initial public offering.

I loved engineering, but I wanted to make a substantial impact on the business. And to do so, I would need a finance background. That led me to pursue a Master's degree in business administration at the Wharton School of Business of the University of Pennsylvania. After Wharton, I worked at the leading management consultancy McKinsey & Company before joining Cisco.

In my 15 years at Cisco, I have run our global professional services business, led worldwide sales and services strategy, helped launch Cisco into emerging countries, and co-led the executive team responsible for the enterprise business that accounts for half of Cisco's sales. I also built the foundation for our some of our first partner programs.

The latter was an especially laborious task that required the renegotiation of more than 800 individual partner contracts. Some days, I wondered if it would have been less tedious to rewrite the U.S. federal tax code.

Today I serve as senior vice president of strategy and planning for worldwide operations, a position that allows me to engage with colleagues from nearly every corner of the company. I am able to work with some of the most remarkable people I have ever met. That includes the very people who are responsible for TelePresence—the technology that brought tears to my mother's eyes.

Like my mother, I continue to marvel at what Cisco can do.

I can only imagine what the next 15 years will bring.

1 —————————————————————

Doing Both

"Even in the remotest times, long preceding the Christian era, the ancients understood the value of dignifying their harbors with impressive works. The Colossus of Rhodes and the Pharaohs of Alexandria were counted among the seven wonders of the world...But the bridge across the Golden Gate would dwarf and overshadow them all."[1]

When James Wilkins wrote these words in an August 1916 editorial for the San Francisco *Call Bulletin*, he was an inspired journalist, an aspiring engineer and a frustrated commuter. The Marin County resident boarded a ferry each day, crossing the increasingly crowded waters of the San Francisco Bay to his office in the city. In an era of automobiles, slow-moving ferries were akin to the horse and buggy. Wilkins knew there had to be a better way.

In the early 1900s, San Francisco was the largest city in the world served primarily by ferries. While other population centers in the United States boomed, San Francisco found its economic growth stymied and its waters clogged with ferry traffic and weary travelers. Ferries simply couldn't keep up with demand or population growth in a city surrounded by water on three sides. Without a sustained link to neighboring communities, the region struggled to grow or connect with outlying communities.

Wilkins' 1916 editorial was a rallying cry. He challenged the beleaguered city, which had only recently rebounded from the brink of collapse after the 1906 earthquake, to build a bridge on the grandest scale. Wilkins envisioned not only a road between San Francisco and Marin County, but a work of art that would rival the world's great achievements in architecture—a monument like no other.

But building a bridge would be a daunting challenge. It would need to span more than 6,700 feet across a strait almost constantly pounded by 60-mile-per-hour winds. A mere 12 miles from the San Andreas Fault, whose tremors nearly decimated San Francisco in 1906, the bridge would certainly need to withstand major seismic activity. It would have to be tall enough to accommodate ships passing underneath its deck. The city's notorious fog would likely slow construction. And the project would need to overcome these obstacles without disturbing the natural beauty of the San Francisco Bay.

Could it be done?

Many had their doubts—but not Chicago native Joseph Strauss, a veteran engineer with hundreds of bridges to his credit.

Strauss initially proposed a combination cantilever and suspension bridge in 1921. Purely utilitarian, his unsightly design was widely derided. "A hybrid monstrosity with little but functionality to recommend," said one critic.[2]

While he spent eight years lobbying for support from governmental officials, local unions, fellow engineers, and eventually the voters who approved a $35 million bond to finance construction, Strauss overhauled the plans.

But he was not alone. While he was the chief engineer and the project's most visible champion, Strauss surrounded himself with a team that had expertise in both structural engineering and aesthetic design.[3]

Engineer Leon Moisseiff joined Strauss after gaining a national reputation for his work on the Manhattan Bridge. Moisseiff was especially well known for his pioneering efforts in deflection theory, which stated that a bridge must flex and bend in the wind to withstand strong gusts. Moisseiff and fellow engineer Charles Alton Ellis applied this theory to the Golden Gate Bridge. Working by telegram from their offices in New York and Chicago, respectively, the two men addressed the seemingly endless series of engineering challenges, eventually designing a bridge that was flexible enough to avoid damage during earthquakes or sustained winds by swinging 27 feet.

Meanwhile, architect Irving Morrow envisioned not just a bridge, but a sculpture that would complement—not undermine or overshadow—the natural beauty of the area. He was responsible for the art deco styling, including the wide towers and expansive lighting. But Morrow's most renowned contribution is the structure's famous red hue (officially known as International Orange). With this coloring, the bridge blends with the surrounding hillside, yet is still visible through San Francisco's legendary fog.

When Strauss combined Morrow's design with Ellis and Moisseiff's engineering, the result was a flexible, single-span, suspension bridge—one that was longer, narrower, lighter, and more graceful than anything the world had ever seen.

This feat of engineering, the Golden Gate Bridge, has now survived for more than 70 years. Upwards of 100,000 cars traverse it each day—more than 40 million per year. But the bridge is a monument renowned not only for transportation capabilities, but also for magnificence. The American Institute of Architects ranked it fifth on its America's Favorite Architectures list in 2007.[4]

The American Society of Civil Engineers named the Golden Gate Bridge one of the Wonders of the Modern World in 1994, stating "[It] combines engineering strength and beauty. It survived the 1989 Loma Prieta earthquake suffering no damage, and in 66 years the bridge has only been shut briefly (longest closure was 3 hours and 27 minutes) to traffic three times due to periods of high sustaining winds. Today, the Golden Gate Bridge remains one of the world's most revered and photographed bridges."[5]

The confluence of two seemingly opposing ideals—beauty and strength—is at the heart of the bridge's iconic status. Could the city of

San Francisco have endangered lives with mediocre engineering? Of course not. Would Strauss's original, no-frills design have been sufficient in carrying cars to and from San Francisco? Perhaps. But would it today be a monument, a tourist attraction and one of the most photographed sites in the world? Unlikely.

When it opened to traffic, the Golden Gate Bridge was the longest single-span suspension bridge in the world, a position it retained for more than 25 years. Seven decades later, it still has the second-longest main span of any suspension bridge in the United States.

Impressive. But a nearby bridge is physically bigger, more heavily trafficked, and a greater marvel of engineering. That is the Bay Bridge. Just five miles east of the Golden Gate, it shuttles more than 270,000 cars each day between Oakland and San Francisco.

Opening just six months before the Golden Gate Bridge, the Bay Bridge is the longest high-level, steel bridge in the world. "Its construction required the greatest expenditure of funds ever used for a single structure in the history of man. Its foundations extend to the greatest depth below water of any bridge built by man; one pier was sunk at 242 feet below water, and another at 200 feet. The deeper pier is bigger than the largest of the Pyramids and required more concrete than the Empire State Building in New York," says University of San Francisco history professor John Bernard McGloin.[6]

Despite this feat of engineering, the prominence of the Bay Bridge is dwarfed by that of its famous neighbor. Just open the photo album of any family that has visited San Francisco. You'll likely find pictures of children smiling back at you from the deck of the Golden Gate Bridge, but not posed in the shadows of the Bay Bridge.

Why the difference?

Rather than focusing on form or function, the Golden Gate Bridge does both. Strauss and his team did not settle for strength or beauty, but instead recognized that each could complement and enhance the other. They bestowed on the bridge both strength and beauty. They did both.

Of course, this concept doesn't just apply to bridges. It holds true in sports, in nature, and in business—in fact, in most aspects of life. Gymnasts need strength and flexibility. Sports teams win with offense and defense. Ecosystems depend on both prey and predators. Car makers focus on safety and performance. Parents give their children roots and wings.

And a successful business prioritizes growth and profitability. Innovation and operational excellence.

In 1984, nearly half a century after the Golden Gate Bridge opened to traffic, one such business opened its doors, mere miles from the famous structure. When its founders needed a name and logo for the fledgling enterprise, they thought of the bridge that represented their city: San Francisco. Shortening the city's name led the founders to their new moniker: Cisco. And the shape of the Golden Gate Bridge—formed by its towers and suspension cables—inspired the Cisco logo. It was certainly appropriate. Much as bridges connect people across a body of water, Cisco's technology connects people and information across a network.

But Cisco took more from the Golden Gate Bridge than a name, a logo, or even the goal of bringing people together. Cisco also transformed itself by leveraging the same principle that has made the Golden Gate Bridge an icon for more than seven decades: Doing Both.

By doing both, Cisco approaches every decision as an opportunity to seize, rather than a sacrifice to endure. This allows the company to avoid a basic trap that ensnarls a lot of companies: the belief that when confronted with two divergent options, an organization must make a difficult trade-off in order to pursue its objectives. The basic premise of this book is that such thinking leads to false choices more often than it produces breakthrough insights. Instead of desired outcomes, it inevitably leads to reduced expectations.

But you can aspire for more.

Instead of choosing one thing to the exclusion of the other, what if you could do both, each for the benefit of the other? Not a balanced

compromise between two objectives, but a mutually reinforcing multiplier in which each side makes the other better. Jim Collins and
Jerry Porras explored this idea in their 1994 book, *Built to Last*. "A
highly visionary company doesn't want to blend yin and yang into a
gray, indistinguishable circle that is neither highly yin nor highly yang;
it aims to be distinctly yin and distinctly yang—both at the same time,
all the time. Irrational? Perhaps. Rare? Yes. Difficult? Absolutely."[7]

Cisco recognizes the wisdom of these words. And it has benefited
handsomely as a result. Over the past seven years, the company has
doubled its revenue, tripled its profits, and quadrupled its earnings
per share. Cisco has more than $40 billion cash on hand and gener-
ated more than $10 billion of annual cash flow in 2009, global reces-
sion notwithstanding. It routinely ranks among the most admired
companies and best places to work around the world. Cisco is one of
the few in technology that caters to customers of all sizes, from individual consumers to the world's largest institutions. Its brand is estimated to be worth $22 billion—the fourteenth most valuable in the
world, according to Interbrand.[8] With each new day, Cisco's influence
grows. In 2009, the company became one of just 30 that comprise the
Dow Jones Industrial Average.

The following chapters explore Cisco's experiences with doing
both. I examine how this has helped the company enter new markets,
introduce breakthrough technologies, scale its operations, engage with
more customers, and better harness the potential of its people.

Perhaps some of our challenges will sound familiar to you. Perhaps they are limiting your organization from reaching its full potential. Perhaps you are struggling to choose between two alternatives
right now.

If so, you just might find a bridge to a whole new world of opportunity in the pages that follow. I invite you to think of that the next
time you face a difficult choice or are vexed by an uncomfortable
compromise. The best answer may surprise you.

Maybe, you just need to do both.

2

New & Improved *and* The Next Big Thing

Sustaining and Disruptive Innovation

When people think of innovation, they tend to envision life-saving medical devices or advanced solar-powered energy panels. Laundry detergent, however, isn't something that typically leaps to mind.

But it does to the men and women of Procter & Gamble (P&G). Their new liquid laundry detergents may never win FDA approval or push the envelope of photovoltaic materials, but they are transforming the way Americans wash their clothes and could someday do the same for consumers in other countries if P&G has its way. That's a big deal considering that the worldwide market for textile cleaning products is expected to grow to $43 billion by 2013, according to Datamonitor.[1] P&G already controls 26.1 percent of the market—the largest share of any single manufacturer—and is now poised to grab even more thanks to its new, disruptive detergent products.

The secret to P&G's influence is "laundry detergent compaction," a technique for compressing ever more cleaning power into ever smaller concentrations. In the early 2000s, P&G perfected a technique that could compact two to three times as much cleaning power into a liquid concentration. That was a remarkable breakthrough that has led to a change not only in consumer shopping habits, but also a revolution in industry supply-chain economics. Here's why.

Consumers love concentrated liquids because they are easier to carry, pour, and store. Retailers, meanwhile, prefer them because they take up less floor and shelf space, which means higher sales-per-square foot—a big deal to Walmart, Target, and others. Shippers and wholesalers, meantime, value reduced-sized products because their smaller bottles translate into reduced fuel consumption and better warehouse space utilization. And environmentalists favor the products because they use less packaging and produce less waste than conventional products.

When first unveiled, company watchers wondered if consumers would be put off by the reduced-sized packages of Tide, Gain, Cheer, and similar products. Their concerns were for naught as consumers snapped them up. P&G was so pleased by the reception that it decided to replace all of its liquid laundry products with compacted versions in 2008. They helped drive sales of fabric and home care products up 6 percent in 2008—a significant jump in a mature market and a down economy that added hundreds of millions to P&G's bottom line.

So how does P&G, a company with more than 170 years of experience behind it, continue to be innovative? The answer is that the Cincinnati-based company has a passion for innovation and a proven process, too.

"We innovate across more categories and on more leading brands than any other consumer products company," says former P&G CEO A.G. Lafley.[2] P&G does that, he says, because the company has a broader range of science and technology than its competitors and invests more in innovation and marketing support than any other consumer products company. This helps P&G deliver an "unrelenting stream of innovation with systematic discipline," he adds.[3]

What distinguishes P&G isn't the mere size of its investment innovation—although it does invest a greater portion of revenue to R&D than rivals Kimberly-Clark and Unilever—but its approach. P&G is one of the few organizations with a process for pursuing both *disruptive* and *sustaining* innovation simultaneously. That gives the company ongoing momentum in the categories in which it currently competes, and lift for entering adjacent markets or transforming existing ones. That's something few companies enjoy because they cannot do both. Because of commitments to existing customers, pressure from investors to deliver short-term results, or even wariness over disrupting existing revenue streams, companies are often reluctant to invest in innovations whose payoff horizons can't accurately be determined.

When this happens, companies find themselves unable to pursue "the next big thing." It's a problem many don't even know they have and yet is perhaps one of the biggest ones they will ever face. This chapter illustrates the differences between disruptive and sustaining innovation, makes the case for doing both, and outlines Cisco's pursuits.

Let's start with basic descriptions of the two distinct types of innovation and what they have contributed in various industries.

Sustaining Innovation: Prolonging Today's Profits with Yesterday's Bold Ideas

Sustaining innovations are the relentless improvements necessary to build on past successes. They make existing products better, faster, or cheaper in the eyes of customers by offering new features and functionality. Honey Nut Cheerios, Boeing's stretch version of the 767, and the all-new Honda Accord are all examples of sustaining innovation.

In addition to providing new product benefits, sustaining innovation protects customer investments, builds employee morale, and helps satisfy investor demands. While sustaining innovations are often developed in response to competitive threats, many often wind up being leapfrog advancements, nonetheless. The zip-locking-style plastic sandwich bag brought to market by Dow Chemical was a sustaining innovation patterned after a pencil bag developed more than a decade earlier. The zip bag eventually overtook flip sandwich bags and now dominates the market.

Disruptive Innovation: Making New Rules for Tomorrow

In comparison to these advances, disruptive innovations and inventions enable companies to create new markets or significantly alter existing ones. They are the rule breakers and the game changers that rivals fear and laggards dread. They make kings of newcomers and paupers of hangers on. They do it by introducing capabilities and functionality never before available and by solving problems that previously went unanswered. Disruptive innovations change where or how value is created and alter the fundamentals of business. When they hit, they have a profound impact on any industry they touch.

Consider the impact of the iPod and iTunes on the entire music industry. Apple's technology drove many consumers to stop buying CDs and instead embrace the disruptive innovation that replaced them: digitized music sold as unglamorous, often inferior-sounding, but infinitely more convenient MP3 files.

As a result of its power, disruptive innovation paves the way for new growth and provides perhaps the only reliable basis for inserting an organization into existing markets where barriers to entry are high and established leaders are entrenched.

The point is that both disruptive and sustaining innovations are vitally important. But it is difficult to pursue both at the same time. Doing so often creates tension in the form of disputes over talent, resources, and priorities. Leaders often find that the two forms of innovation require very different oversight and metrics, as well as best practices. As a result, many pursue one form of innovation over the other. But that only results in lost opportunity. For example, Polaroid, once one of America's most storied innovators, filed for bankruptcy in 2008. The company that made instant gratification through photography possible was upended by a disruptive force itself: digital imagery. By clinging to film and outdated cameras, the company sealed its own fate and lost out as digital camera makers took over. Polaroid did unveil a line of digital cameras in 2008, but it's unclear whether the company will ever be the innovative force it once was.

Polaroid isn't the only company to falter because of an inability to produce both sustaining and disruptive innovations. Parallel examples can be found in an array of industries including automobiles, airlines, clothing and retail. What's amazing is the number of instances in which corporate giants have been out-maneuvered by smaller, more nimble players, despite owning some of the same disruptive ideas that eventually upended them. Technology giant Motorola, for example, missed two critical product transitions in the mobile phone industry. In the early 1990s, the company was slow to evolve its product line from analog to digital devices, opening the door for Nokia to establish itself as the new market leader. A decade later, Motorola stumbled again when mobile phones shifted to fully upgradable, software-based smart phones, providing an opportunity for Apple, Blackberry, and others to take additional market share.

Why can't big companies simultaneously produce disruptive and sustaining innovations? It is a vexing question that has been studied endlessly in the past decade, especially since the publication of Clayton Christensen's 1997 best-seller, *The Innovator's Dilemma*. In that book, Christensen chronicles the struggles of big, successful companies that spend their time and energy on existing products, revenue streams, and profits to the near exclusion of the next big thing. When game-changing innovation arrives on the scene from another competitor, or even from within their own organizations, big companies often struggle to form an appropriate response.[4]

Organizations have tried to overcome this challenge, albeit with mixed results. One model is to create a discrete team inside a larger organization for the nurturing of disruptive innovation. Well-known examples are Bell Labs (later known as Alcatel-Lucent Bell Labs), IBM Research, Microsoft Research, and Xerox Palo Alto Research Center

(PARC). The results? Hit or miss. Many of the innovations that sprang forth from these efforts were never commercialized because the organizations that produced them were unable to routinely adopt them.

A more recent model is popular with companies like Google, 3M, and Motorola. These companies ask employees to devote a certain amount of their working hours to generating disruptive ideas. The challenge with this model is capturing the big ideas that engineers or scientists generate. Without structure, good ideas often languish in these informal arrangements. Furthermore, the approach runs counter to the creative process that produces the bulk of disruptive innovation—relentless, unfettered pursuit of an idea. Because of this, Google, for example, recently added a layer of managerial oversight to ensure that good ideas didn't slip away.[5]

While the former model isolates disruptive innovation, the latter opens it up to the masses. As evidenced by the limited success of each, neither approach is optimized for *both* disruptive *and* sustaining innovation. Because of this, most organizations tend to fall back on the familiar refrains of sustaining innovation.

That's what happened to one-time technology high-flyer Iomega Corp. A decade and a half ago, the Roy, Utah, company was a darling of the technology industry for its breakthrough, disruptive innovation: the Zip drive. Zip drives and their accompanying Zip disks simplified the process of backing up electronic files and transferring them between computers. One year after its 1995 launch, Iomega's annual sales nearly quadrupled to $1.2 billion. The sleepy stock skyrocketed from $2 to more than $80 per share.

But, as often happens to disruptive innovators, Iomega found itself struggling with Christensen's dilemma. Not eager to give up its lucrative franchise, the company devoted its energies to producing sustained enhancements to its disk storage products. But the market was moving on. Soon, Iomega's sales sputtered, and a stock slide followed. Try as it might to revive its fortunes, Iomega's attempts at sustained innovation were no match for disruptive technologies, including writeable CDs and Flash drives.

As late as 2001, Iomega was still hoping for Zip to soar once more: "In a world where technology is often obsolete by the time it gets to market, the Zip drive is a rare prize: technology so reliable and versatile that it's a core ingredient in virtually every new Iomega product," the company touted in its 2000 Annual Report.[6] Just one year later, however, a new management team conceded that the company was "troubled" and that new efforts to revive Iomega were floundering. "Looking back over the year, we can now see that our wounds, for the most part, were self-inflicted," the team told investors at year's end.[7] The problem: The company simply couldn't produce anything as disruptively innovative as the original Zip drive nor could it produce sustaining innovation in sufficient quantity to keep customers from defecting to other products. Unable to recreate the magic for Zip technology, Iomega's management team eventually sold the company to EMC in 2008 for $200 million, a small fraction of what Iomega was once worth.

A New Model for a New Era

Things could have turned out differently for Iomega, Polaroid, and others if only they had a process for pursuing both disruptive and sustaining innovation. P&G has such a model, and it consistently produces benefits for the company. This includes the "Corporate Innovation Fund," an in-house venture capital arm that provides money to test high-risk, high-reward ideas to determine if they warrant additional resources. And the P&G "FutureWorks" business unit focuses exclusively on innovations that can create new businesses around the world.

Like P&G, Cisco believes the simultaneous pursuit of sustaining and disruptive innovation is one of the most important missions a company can undertake. The key is to pursue both with equal vigor and use each for the benefit of the other.

Some background: In fiscal 2008, Cisco invested $5.2 billion, or 13.2 percent of revenue, in research and development. This is in line with other technology leaders, including Intel (16.4 percent) and Microsoft (13.5 percent).

The organization at Cisco responsible for this investment is the Cisco Development Organization (CDO). CDO innovates in a number of areas including core networking, video, virtualization software, and collaboration, among others. This work involves products familiar to many Cisco followers and technologies many don't realize Cisco pursues. That includes microprocessors, for example. Surprising as it sounds, Cisco is one of the world's leading semiconductor design houses for high-complexity designs. In fact, its designs rival those of the world leader in microprocessors, Intel.

Consider: The two benchmarks used to routinely describe the complexity of a chip are the number of cores it contains and the number of transistors on it. At the time of this writing, Intel's latest high-end microprocessor, the Core i7, contains up to 8 cores per chip. That's a lot. But it's not as many as Cisco's Quantum Flow Processor, which boasts 40 cores on a single chip, operating at 1.2 gigahertz. What does that mean in laymen's terms? While Intel and Cisco are solving two different problems, imagine a device that has the power to search through every book ever written in every language in a single hour. That's the power of the Quantum Flow Processor, which is the heart of Cisco's Aggregation Services Router (ASR).

Cisco Senior Vice Presidents Tony Bates, Kathy Hill, and Pankaj Patel are tasked with developing both disruptive and sustaining innovation. For years, their track record has been impressive. Sustaining innovations, for example, have inspired customers who used rival products to buy Cisco for the first time, improved the loyalty of existing customers, and helped the company launch into adjacent markets. Sustaining innovation is also responsible for keeping Cisco's gross margins above 60 percent for years longer than experts ever thought the company could.

Take Ethernet switching, for example. Cisco gradually refined its Ethernet switches to the point where they became the number one choice among customers for connectivity in office environments. After achieving this market position, Cisco saw an opportunity to expand its influence to include other types of networking devices, including wireless access points. This was in addition to connecting the servers, PCs, and laptops that customers were adding to their networks by the millions. The new devices, however, often lacked a power source of their own and thus could not be added to IP networks without some enhancements, which Cisco added. This sustaining innovation opened the door to Unified Communications, a category of products that help customers save billions on communications costs while improving the usefulness of devices on which they already rely.

This effort also set the stage for a whole new class of products that manage power consumption. This feat could not have been timed better, given the current push to reduce energy costs and invest in more environmentally-friendly technologies. With Cisco EnergyWise-compliant products, customers can centrally power-on and power-off network devices on an as-needed basis. That not only includes traditional data and communications gear, but also products that previously ran over other networks, including heating and cooling devices, lighting systems, and security equipment. Cisco's innovation made the company a more important player in markets far removed from its traditional base, enabling it to leapfrog competitors and open up new opportunities.

In addition to its success in sustaining innovation, Cisco wanted to accelerate disruptive innovation in a more predictable fashion. Some of the steps Cisco took to pursue both disruptive and sustaining innovation are detailed throughout the remainder of this chapter. These efforts required Cisco to try two new and different ideas, one for tapping the best thinking outside the company, and another for making the most of the best ideas originating inside Cisco. The first idea was an attempt to pursue external venturing in the form of "spin-ins," while the latter was a plan to pursue internal venturing via the creation of a new business unit.

Here's how these efforts turned out.

External Venturing: Invent Like a Startup, Scale Like a Giant

Because it is based in California's famed Silicon Valley, home to countless innovators that changed the IT industry, Cisco can't help but notice the wealth of creativity and energy in its own backyard. Without going too deep into the lore of Silicon Valley, it's worth noting that the area is an ideal place to start a company. It is home to world-class engineers, moneyed venture capitalists, ambitious entrepreneurs, and seasoned professionals from the worlds of engineering, law, public relations, marketing, sales, and just about any other discipline a company needs to thrive. The area is a perfect incubator for producing disruptive innovations.

Cisco, itself, is a perfect example. Founded in 1984 by Stanford University scientists, the disruptive technologies Cisco brought to market changed the way the world communicates and collaborates.

But somewhere along the way, Cisco started acting less like a hungry startup and more like an established market leader. It was bound to happen, especially after the company blew past the $1 billion, $5 billion, and $10 billion annual sales thresholds.

As Cisco grew into a large corporation, its leaders began to worry that the company was producing more sustaining innovation than disruptive innovation. But why? After all, Cisco had world-class engineers and brilliant thinkers, just like many of the promising startups in San Jose. The more Cisco studied the issue, the more it became clear that the answer lay within its own walls. Business processes honed to a fine point were actually hindering the development of disruptive innovation. Like a force of nature,

Cisco's best practices systematically wiped out nonstandard thinking and nourished only those ideas that produced immediate returns.

In many instances, this was simply good business, leading to gains in profit and market share. But these practices didn't foster the creativity or flexibility that breakthrough ideas often require. The more Cisco focused on improving existing products, the less bandwidth it had for disruptive innovation. That frustrated company leaders, who valued the power of revolutionary thinking. It's a problem that happens at a lot of big companies. Even on the rare occasion when an established organization does prioritize a disruptive technology, often as result of an ephemeral infatuation by a senior executive, it fails to put into place the culture and processes required for nurturing disruptive innovations.

Much like author Christensen, Cisco's leadership team understood this. It therefore sought out disruptive innovation in quick-moving start-ups that weren't burdened by Wall Street expectations or legacy customer requirements. These companies could pursue ideas without fear of cannibalizing existing product lines or disappointing traditional customers. Since its early days, Cisco has always been poised to acquire the next great producer of disruptive technology.

Of course, the problem with looking to outside companies for breakthrough ideas is the uncertainty that goes along with it. When considering an acquisition, Cisco studies the quality of the incoming leadership team, the culture of the company, and the uniqueness of its technologies. Are they truly breakthrough? Are they sustainably differentiated? Can they be commercialized quickly? These are but a handful of the questions Cisco considers. Yet despite this due diligence and its well-documented success with acquisitions, Cisco takes a risk—an expensive risk—with every deal.

What if Cisco could reduce this uncertainty by getting involved with companies at an earlier stage? Wouldn't that better position it to tap the entrepreneurial spirit of startups? Many inside the company began to wonder.

This thinking led Cisco to pursue disruptive innovation via external venturing, or spin-ins. A spin-in is similar to a traditional acquisition save for few notable differences. In a spin-in, Cisco makes an early-stage investment in a company in return for special considerations. These include the option to purchase the company if and when pre-determined customer and sales milestones are met, and the right to provide management oversight, where appropriate. In some instances, Cisco will also transfer some key employees to the spin-in candidate and provide additional guidance to help nurture the company along.

Because of the unique nature of spin-ins, they provide the best of all worlds: the energy, creativity, and passion of a startup, plus the scale, management savvy, market access, and financial strength of an established powerhouse. When evaluating spin-in candidates, Cisco looks for disruptive technology that adheres to its technology standards, products that fit with its business model, and innovation that meets the specific needs of its customers. The purchase price of a spin-in is tied to the performance milestones it reaches, thus reducing the risk of an acquisition for Cisco.

For all their merit, however, spin-ins are not always the easiest way to pursue disruptive innovation. That's especially true when there are former employees to repatriate back into the main company after a spin-in is complete. In exchange for their willingness to take some risk with their careers, Cisco will, for example, monetarily reward employees who transfer to the spin-in upon reintegration. These and other arrangements, however, can lead to morale problems if not handled appropriately.

In addition, spin-ins can take longer to complete than a traditional acquisition. Incubation could take a long time, even though integration tends to be quick. If time-to-market is an issue or a completely new business model is required, Cisco often will opt for a traditional acquisition rather than a spin-in. But if the goal is disruptive innovation around areas adjacent to Cisco's markets and time-to-market is not the overriding factor, the spin-in model can be powerful.

Spin-ins are appealing not only to Cisco, but also to the start-up company itself. With an established company providing financial help and managerial oversight, a startup is more likely to succeed. Among other things, a large backer can help a startup to align its technology with market needs and partner capabilities. With financing, operational and go-to-market concerns minimized, spin-in candidates can doggedly pursue engineering objectives.

In 2008, CEO John Chambers summarized his thinking on why the spin-in model is ideal for helping a company bring disruptive innovation to market: "The advantage of a spin-in is that you can jointly develop well-integrated products by closely sharing your technology, expertise, and product roadmaps. The acquired technologies of a spin-in become part of Cisco's technology architecture in a much shorter time than with traditional acquisition methods. Secondly, a spin-in allows Cisco to tie an acquisition price to product revenues and the margins associated with those revenues. This results-oriented approach avoids the typical challenges of estimating the value of an acquisition."[8]

Because of these and other benefits, Cisco has pursued spin-ins with vigor since the mid-1990s. They have helped launch the company into adjacent markets—often with ideas that were more disruptive than what it was pursuing internally. Take storage technology, for example.

In the early 2000s, storage was becoming ever more important to enterprise customers. Every application they used, from email to ERP systems to databases, required its own dedicated storage solution. That was a problem for IT planners, who had to allocate an ever-increasing portion of their budget to islands of storage devices with each passing year. Frustrated by their inability to predict exact storage needs, they tended to over-buy to ensure capacity. Because these devices were connected to Cisco networks, Cisco could see a market opportunity in helping customers consolidate, virtualize, and manage their storage devices by sharing them across the network. When it posed this idea to customers, they overwhelmingly responded, "Yes!"

Storage area networking was exactly the kind of market Cisco loved: It was big, adjacent to the networking market, undergoing a transition and highly relevant to customers. Cisco leaders knew that profits awaited the company that could help customers solve this problem. The company just needed a disruptive innovation.

That led Cisco to Andiamo, an early developer of intelligent storage networking technology, which enabled customers to consolidate disparate devices onto a single, secure, integrated platform. This promised to save money through greater utilization of storage devices and on administration costs.

Cisco invested in Andiamo in early 2001 and finalized the deal in February 2004. By then, Andiamo was earning $130 million in annual sales—a staggering accomplishment for a company that was just three years old. The reason, says Andiamo co-founder and Cisco executive Mario Mazzola, was because Cisco's experienced veterans were able to partner with the technologically savvy startup to ramp up sales, engineering, marketing, customer support, and manufacturing—all of the disciplines required for a company to succeed. In the five years since the acquisition, the technology originally developed by Andiamo has continued to play a critical role for Cisco beyond storage. Its software, for example, now serves as the operating system for the Cisco Nexus 7000 Series Switch. And Cisco now has more than 50% share in the high-end modular storage market.

Capitalizing on the success of Andiamo, Cisco would soon use the spin-in model again—this time, for one of its biggest gambles yet: virtualized data centers.

Data centers are essentially the hub of all business computing. They house racks of servers that manage the flow of information and communications for big organizations. These servers do everything from crunch financials to store data to provision applications. A typical large company spends a large percentage of its IT budget on maintaining its data center. In other words, Cisco customers spend billions of dollars to manage a growing, complex, and often inflexible infrastructure.

Cisco saw a better way, especially after its initial foray into the data center with storage innovations. It believed that the triad of networking, storage, and virtualization technology could blend data center requirements on a virtualized server, thereby reducing cost and complexity. Cisco knew it was just a matter of time before a competitor capitalized on this opportunity, and it didn't have the structure to pursue such innovations internally.

But one startup did.

The company was Nuova, a San Jose startup specializing in high-performance, data center infrastructure equipment. Like Andiamo, Nuova offered a disruptive innovation that utilized the Cisco networking architecture. Its virtualization technology transformed how big pieces of networking and computing gear shared communications and information resources and offered customers another way to consolidate vendors and reduce their costs.

Cisco first invested in Nuova in August 2006 and bought it outright in April 2008. Today, the company's technologies form the basis of the Cisco Unified Computing System, Cisco's initial foray into the virtualized computing market. Only time will tell if the move will pay off, but early indicators are positive.

"Revolutionary. Cutting edge. State of the art. These words and phrases are bandied around for so very many products in the IT field that they become useless, bland, expected. The truth is that truly revolutionary products are few and far between. That said, Cisco's Unified Computing System fits the bill," said technology journal *InfoWorld* in November 2009.[9]

The rewards that Cisco reaps from spin-ins are undeniable. This is rooted in an unwavering focus on customer success, rather than internal metrics. Cisco, for example, measures and incents its spin-in candidates based on the delivery of solutions that meet specific customer needs and drive revenue, rather than just technical milestones. This customer-centricity guarantees market relevance and focuses the collective team on a set of shared goals.

As attractive as disruptive innovation is, it's not an end unto itself. The real multiplier effect occurs when it is paired with sustaining innovation. Cisco looks for its disruptive and sustaining innovations to drive one another whenever possible (see Figure 2.1). The Nuova and Andiamo spin-ins, for example, facilitated this cross-leverage many times over. Innovations in Cisco's switching products helped the company create disruptive innovation in the storage market, which in turn accelerated the next generation of switching. This enabled the company to enter the unified computing marketplace.

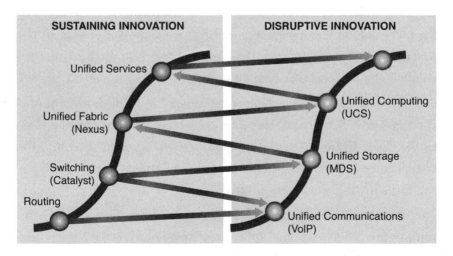

Figure 2.1   Doing both—sustaining and disruptive innovation

Spin-ins have dramatically accelerated Cisco's disruptive innovation engine, gaining the company entry into key markets like voice, storage, and computing. As promising as external venturing is, however, it only forms half of Cisco's disruptive innovation equation. The other half comes from within.

Internal Venturing: Rebels of the World, Unite

With external venturing beginning to pay dividends, Cisco looked inward to see if it could mine untapped disruptive ideas. Doing that within the confines of the engineering organization proved difficult, however, given the organization's focus on exploiting the potential of existing products. So Cisco created the Emerging Technologies Group (ETG). Its primary mission is to pursue disruptive, new ideas that could grow into $1 billion market opportunities within 5 to 7 years of launch.

Given the amount of effort required to take an idea from zero to $1 billion, the ETG needed a unique charter within the CDO. Rather than a shadow R&D unit, Cisco ETG is an incubation center where innovative ideas are translated into business opportunities, not just patents or scientific breakthroughs. Despite its small size in comparison to the rest of the CDO, ETG is responsible for some of the company's highest profile engineering projects, and its leader reports directly to the CEO.

Given its unique charter, Cisco thought long and hard about whom to appoint to lead the ETG. In addition to a world-class technologist, company executives believed the group needed a leader who could anticipate business trends and harness ingenuity without stifling creativity. They wanted an individual with the heart of a company loyalist and the soul of an independent entrepreneur.

One candidate in particular stood out: Marthin de Beer.

A native of South Africa, de Beer moved to the United States in 1993 to pursue a career in Silicon Valley. The founder of two successful startups in his native land, de Beer eventually found his way to Cisco in 1995.

Upon joining the company, de Beer worked in the switching organization, a large and rapidly growing part of the company in the late 1990s. While he welcomed the benefits and stability that the big company provided, he nonetheless pined for the energy and inspiration that an entrepreneurial environment offered.

When the opportunity arose to lead Cisco's efforts in voice technology, de Beer accepted. Instead of driving a technology that had great momentum and company-wide support, de Beer found himself advocating one that had yet to generate much acceptance across the company. To create momentum, de Beer pursued a simple strategy that revolved around the following: Get along with others, find rabid fans, and develop some lighthouse customer accounts. It worked like a charm.

Opportunity knocked again in 2004. Former head of engineering Charlie Giancarlo needed a leader who could jump start Cisco Tele-Presence, a high-definition video collaboration solution. Despite Cisco's engineering prowess, Giancarlo recognized that the disruptive innovation needed for this venture was fundamentally *different* than the sustaining innovation CDO typically produced. It required different people, different processes, and even different tools for motivating employees. That meant creating a new team.

de Beer seemed like the right leader, but he was hesitant. Giving up his 1,500-person organization to run a previously untested start-up unit inside the company was a big risk. He even wondered if he was being driven out of the company. "Come on Charlie, just tell me if I'm fired," he said. But Giancarlo reiterated his goal: to create startups from *within* the company. An engineer at heart, de Beer knew that most ideas failed to turn into commercially viable ventures. What if ours don't pan out, he wondered? After two weeks of debating the offer, he put his concerns aside. "I'll take the job," he told Giancarlo, "but on one condition: it's okay for me to fail; I know I won't always succeed."

"It's okay if you fail," Giancarlo responded, "as long as you don't fail too often or for the wrong reasons."

Ultimately, the two agreed that up to three out of every four ideas might fail. But that was still better than the rate of failure among typical Silicon Valley startups. With a hand-picked team and support from other parts of the company, they could very well come up with some big hits, they agreed. So the Emerging Technologies Group (ETG) was born. It had the express mission of creating a pipeline of new ideas and a process for bringing them to market in a repeatable fashion.

"The entire ETG was created to develop solutions for markets that are adjacent to existing opportunities and hence more revolutionary in nature," says de Beer.

Because ETG is chartered with developing "disruptive innovations" and not mere "products," its approach differs from that of a typical product development team inside Cisco. In fact, the entire creation of the ETG was a major cultural evolution for Cisco. The composition of the team, the way it was measured, and even the processes they used to develop products were different than for Cisco. For example, the development of Cisco TelePresence began with cardboard boxes and foam blocks, not electronic cameras, computers, and digital screens. ETG approached video collaboration from a fresh perspective.

As a result, "Cisco TelePresence is a complete experience shift, not just a new technology," says Phil Graham, a vice president with Cisco's ETG and one of the principal architects behind TelePresence. "We had to think of it down to what the user would experience, down to every last detail." That included things never before incorporated into Cisco technology, including furniture and paint color for the walls in TelePresence rooms. That's because part of the Cisco Tele-Presence experience is a conference table with an invisible horizon that melds perfectly with another table visible on a computer screen in life-like color, size, and shape. If ETG had not thought through all of these softer aspects, the entire Cisco TelePresence value proposition—the ability to conduct a virtual meeting with multiple people located in different places around the globe as though they were all assembled in the same room—would have been lost. Consider: Prior to releasing the product, a debate was waged inside the company. Should TelePresence cameras include the ability to zoom, Cisco leaders wondered? Ultimately, the company decided against a zoom feature because, as one engineer put it, "humans can't zoom in person."

What else did Cisco ETG do differently? It assembled a team in a very un-Cisco-like way. To create ETG, Cisco looked inside for proven leaders who were known to have a rebellious streak. Company executives wanted loyalists, but also independent, free thinkers. And they didn't necessarily want engineers to run the organization. Take ETG's chief technology officer Guido Jouret, for example. His background is in IT systems management, not product development. The same is true of Charles Stucki, who joined ETG as the VP of emerging technologies incubation and eventually became the general manager of the TelePresence Systems Business Unit (TSBU). His background is in business consulting, not start-up development. He was hired to provide customer and industry perspective that helps Cisco develop more exacting solutions for specific challenges. Later, he developed the framework that helped ETG replicate its successes and systematize its approach to developing ideas.

Worth noting are some of the would-be leaders that ETG rejected. Some big thinkers volunteered to join ETG but were passed over due to their perceived inability to put ideas through a process that would result in disruptive business opportunities. Cisco also wanted to seed ETG with a diverse mix of "white hats"—chosen for their ability to see potential in ideas—and "black hats," who are good at identifying shortcomings and potential stumbling blocks.

Then there was the question of how much money to give to ETG. Jouret jokes that the company's management team starved it on purpose. Senior executives decided that a hungry team short on time and short on funds would work to accomplish things faster. So ETG was forced to subsist on the leanest of budgetary diets. Its fiscal year 2008 budget was just 2.8 percent of the total Cisco R&D expenditure. Nevertheless, it is more than what many Silicon Valley venture capitalists spend in a given year, Jouret notes, and enough to get things done if the money is well spent. The key is focus. And that's why new business processes are critical.

As with all processes at Cisco, ETG starts with the customer in mind. Engineers are required to meet with no less than 30 customers before they pursue a new idea.

"We do not ask customers what they want. That too often leads to incremental improvements over what they have experienced. Instead we focus on the customer's role and what they seek to accomplish. We also meet with non-customers—that is, organizations that are not currently buyers of products and services in the category that we are targeting. This helps us produce truly disruptive innovations," says de Beer.

From the beginning, ETG was consumed by chasing new ideas. Its engineers were encouraged to focus maniacally on their projects at hand. That meant disregarding noncritical conference calls, refusing extraneous assignments, and declining outside speaking requests. That was a radical cultural break inside Cisco, where responsiveness and professional courtesy are deeply ingrained in the company's culture.

Though ETG represented a cultural shift for Cisco, the group did adopt elements of Cisco's culture and make them their own. From the start, ETG embraced Cisco's collaborative mentality, for example. Knowing that Cisco's own engineers were likely sitting on a mountain of great ideas buried under a pile of day-to-day obligations, ETG created I-Zone, an internal, online community where any employee could share, discuss, and hone new product ideas. This framework would enable ETG to transcend organizational, geographical, and even functional boundaries to mine for new ideas. Since its launch in August 2006, employees have submitted in excess of 1,500 ideas to I-Zone.

To tap the creativity that lay beyond its borders, Cisco created a competition called "I-Prize," which provided company outsiders a means to share their ideas with Cisco. Thanks to heavy promotion on YouTube, Facebook, and other social networking sites, the I-Prize competition attracted more than 2,500 people from 104 countries. During a three-month period, they submitted more than 1,100 ideas, 10 percent of which were deemed worthy of serious consideration. After an initial review, the field was narrowed to 12 finalists representing 10 countries and five continents. Finalists were given an opportunity to pitch their ideas directly to a panel of Cisco executives. In October 2008, Cisco named a team from Germany and Russia as the winners of the competition. They were given a $250,000 prize and offered an opportunity to work at Cisco to pursue their breakthrough idea, which, not surprisingly, revolved around a business plan for using IP technology to improve energy efficiency.

To help vet ideas generated from I-Prize and I-Zone, Cisco turned to some of its highest-performing company directors for additional support. Through the Cisco Action Learning Forum (ALF), these directors helped vet proposals and stress-test them for their potential in a rather unique way. Directors were assigned to teams and challenged to translate compelling ideas into a business plan in just three month's time. Chosen for the level of commitment and passion they demonstrated on previous assignments, the directors worked night and day to identify a target market for new ideas, assess the competitive landscape, and come up with a go-to-market strategy, among other things. Afterwards, these directors presented their business plans to senior executives in much the same way start-up companies present their ideas to venture capitalists in Silicon Valley. Cisco funded the best of these ideas and created businesses around them.

To ensure that homegrown and outside ideas were properly evaluated, ETG developed a unique process for identifying, evaluating, incubating, and then launching or rejecting them. The systematic process eliminated a lot of guesswork and made it easier for Cisco to evaluate ideas not on the passions of their creators, but on their potential for producing commercially viable disruptive innovation.

There are specific actions that Cisco will take to nurture an idea from one phase of development to the next (see Figure 2.2).

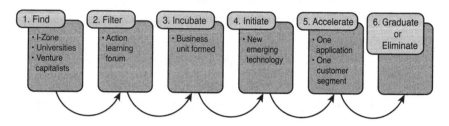

Figure 2.2   Internal venture framework

Unlike the approach taken by other incubation teams in the industry, Cisco ETG keeps new businesses in incubation until they reach $100–$200 million in sales. (Other companies typically hand their new, "big things" over to traditional sales departments much earlier, in some cases when new opportunities reach $10 million in revenue.) But Cisco, which believes its ETG innovations should meet a much broader set of criteria than a simple sales figure, has established a dedicated ETG sales force, which consists of new product and category experts. Though it coordinates with the traditional sales and channels organizations, the ETG sales force remains independent and reports to de Beer, rather than to the Cisco sales leaders. Just like a startup, this ensures that ETG salespeople remain fully dedicated to driving Emerging Technologies. And eventually this approach ensures a smoother transition and integration into the mainstream Cisco organization.

"We track progress against key stage gates and milestones across the entire incubation process. Such progress is an important consideration in evaluating and adjusting our strategy, and in determining whether to proceed to the next phase," says de Beer.[10]

Surprisingly, Cisco will not sell ETG products to just any customer before they graduate. Customers must be prequalified, based on their understanding of the limitations of early-stage products. The reason is simple: New products won't have all features to satisfy all customers.

Cisco therefore selects the customers for whom the initial set of features will meet or exceed their requirements. Rather than tire kickers, Cisco looks for lighthouse accounts that can embrace and then showcase disruptive Cisco innovation, serving as a lighthouse for others to see. In short, ETG looks for customers that demonstrate a similar, pioneering mindset—early adopters, if you will. To help identify these customers, Cisco pushes customers to look inward and ask how they would justify such a purchase and how much they would pay for disruptive innovations.

The approach seems to be working.

ETG sales increased nearly nine-fold between 2007 and 2009. The team has created or identified nine disruptive opportunities. Three are already in the market today and achieving significant success. Each represents a $1 billion-plus opportunity within seven years. Four more are staffed and in the early stages of incubation (gathering customer feedback, refining the market focus, and developing the appropriate solutions), while another has been terminated.

And whatever happened to those cardboard boxes and blocks of foam?

In early 2010, ETG graduated TelePresence and integrated it back into Cisco's mainstream operations. Today, the technology is one of the company's fastest-growing products.

One reason ETG works as a business unit is because the ETG team understood what trust, incentives, and structure could do to help propel them. It established trust by creating a culture that allowed for failures. It also created incentives that worked for start-ups—think realistic profit expectations for units operating in "investment" mode—and developed a structure that invited participation and discouraged complacency.

Innovation Syncopation

Clearly, the decision to pursue spin-ins and incubation simultaneously helped Cisco establish a leadership position in disruptive innovation. Clayton Christensen even picked Cisco as the Disrupter of the Decade in January 2010. "Everything that is done over the Internet is enabled by [Cisco], and they are not done yet," he says.[11]

Disruptive innovation through spin-ins launched the company into the voice, storage, and computing markets with Ardent, Andiamo, and Nuova, respectively. And incubation through ETG helped Cisco take a commanding position in enterprise video. But these are just two of Cisco's approaches to generating sustaining and disruptive innovation through internal and external venturing (see Figure 2.3).

Lower risk Lower reward Lower urgency		Higher risk Higher reward Higher urgency	
Internal		*External*	
Develop	**Incubate**	**Spin-In**	**Acquire**
• Parent company has requisite expertise • New technology is (or needs to be) closely related to existing products	• Close adjacency to core business • Leverage the parent company's technologies	• Further away from the core business • More flexibility in rewards • Greater secrecy required	• Acquired company has established market and/or technical expertise • Extreme flexibility in rewards

Figure 2.3   Internal versus external venturing

But what is the best approach? The answer depends on what your organization is trying to accomplish.

Cisco, for example, has gained from each. But it chooses between them based on specific conditions. When a new idea has significant synergy with existing products or go-to-market strategies, Cisco will incubate the idea internally. Alternatively, the company often looks outside its walls when it wants to pursue something that is very different or unfamiliar.

Difficult as it is, Cisco resists the temptation that pulls down many companies of its size—the notion that they have to develop everything internally. Likewise, it rejects the idea that a small startup is the only way to produce something ingenious. Freed from the gravitational pull that tends to draw mature companies in one direction and newcomers in another, Cisco is able to pick the best from inside and outside to create a compelling and complementary portfolio of products and services.

With this, Cisco can bring to market both disruptive and sustaining innovations to produce transformative value. To ensure that its breakthrough TelePresence solution gained market acceptance, for example, Cisco had to make it easy to use. So the company turned to Call Manager—a sustaining innovation that it developed to run phone calls over the Internet. With this, a sales director in New York can host a live meeting with a customer in Shanghai with just the touch of a button.

The marriage of a disruptive solution with a sustaining technology didn't just fuel sales. It is changing the way people communicate.

Doing both never looked or sounded so good.

3

Current Accounts *and* Future Conquests

Existing and New Business Models

For years, industry watchers have been betting on which company would produce the first reliable, plug-in, electric-powered car. Most experts assumed it would be whichever auto manufacturer first developed a battery powerful enough to run its cars. Would it be General Motors and its Chevy Volt? Or maybe Tesla Motors' Model S?

As it turns out, the pundits may have gotten things backwards. If all goes according to plan, battery-maker BYD could be the first company to deliver a mass-produced, electric-powered, plug-in vehicle, ahead of Detroit, Stuttgart, or Tokyo.

If you don't know the company, open the back of your mobile phone. Chances are the battery powering the device was produced by BYD, a 15-year old company based in Shenzhen, China. Today, BYD is the leading supplier of batteries to Nokia, Samsung, and Motorola. Now it wants to be the leading supplier of power plants for a family of sedans, sub-compacts, and sports coupes that will bear its name. It's no joke. Already BYD has attracted quite a following. Among those interested in the company: Warren Buffet, who plunked down more than $200 million to buy 10 percent of BYD in 2008.

To achieve its aims and provide a return for its backers, BYD has had to overcome vast challenges. It spent 10 years, for example, developing a battery that can power a car from 0 to 60 miles per hour in eight seconds and travel more than 100 miles when fully charged.

And as early as 2003, it began acquiring manufacturing capacity and design expertise.

So why even try? Opportunity. The market for cars is on the cusp of an immense transition—from gas guzzlers to fuel-efficient and environmentally friendly vehicles. BYD, naturally, senses a once-in-a-lifetime chance to shake up the established world order. Newcomers, BYD leaders believe, have as good a shot at capturing the market. And what an opportunity it could be: According to various estimates, the worldwide market for electric vehicles could be as large as 10 million cars per year by 2016. That's more than 12 percent of the global market for automobiles.[1] "It's almost hopeless for a latecomer like us to compete with GM and other established auto makers with a century of experience in gasoline engines," says BYD's wildly ambitious founder and chairman, Wang Chuanfu. "With electric vehicles, we're all at the same starting line."

To get to that starting line, Wang had to embrace a completely new business model to complement its existing model, something that is nearly impossible for most companies. To make the leap from invisible components to branded products, BYD had to develop a new workforce, create a consumer brand, ramp up government relations to engage national safety commissions, and create an entirely new supply chain. Any one of these can bury a company looking to augment its business model. And for good reason: These are extremely difficult challenges to overcome, all the more so in mature industries with high barriers to entry.

Despite the difficulty, some companies persevere. They do so because they believe new business models are the key to enormous value in the form of access to new markets, customers, investment capital, and profits.

This chapter highlights the benefits that can be derived from adopting new business models. It analyzes several companies that have successfully developed them, as well as a few that have tried and failed. It also analyzes the steps Cisco took to implement new business models and the lessons it learned along the way.

Let's start by providing a glimpse into the world of those who have mastered the art of the "new business model" and those who have not. Take Disney, for example. Within the "Magic Kingdom" are theme parks, television networks, cruise ships, merchandising operations, and film studios, among other interests. Though they have different financial models, success metrics, and fundamentals, they nonetheless provide Disney an unrivaled footprint in entertainment.

Most companies never achieve anything close to this level of diversification. That includes some of the biggest and most successful companies on the planet. Many have tried and found it more difficult than previously thought. Take Google, for example.

Google has one of the most enviable business models—search-based advertising—of any company today. But its fortunes remain wholly dependent on that model, leaving it vulnerable to new competitors, market changes, or other challenges. Recognizing this, the company has tried to diversify its business for years. To help spur the development of new ideas, company leaders have gone so far as to encourage Google engineers to spend up to one day per week on open-ended projects that might lead to new business models or innovations. Several promising ideas have sprung from this approach, including the company's Gmail messaging platform and its Google Apps software platform. Despite this, however, Google has yet to diversify its business model and thus remains dependent on its cash cow, which accounts for more than 95 percent of the company's sales.

Given the unprecedented rise of Google in the global marketplace—it commands 71 percent of the search-based advertising market[2]—why should it bother with multiple business models? Because multiple business models provide a company a buffer against downturns in any one sector and an extra lift when times are good. They provide entry into adjacent markets and thus expand a company's opportunity and preserve its longevity should one of its revenue streams come under threat from increased competition, regulatory changes, or even internal challenges. This is especially true of companies with broad portfolios of assets that can be combined to create new value.

IBM, for example, is weathering the 2008–2009 recession better than most tech giants because of this very reason. Its earnings actually increased while those of Dell and Intel fell by double digits. That's because IBM began diversifying its business a decade before the recession crippled the global economy. Since 2000, for example, the company has purchased 40 software companies. It also expanded its services and consulting business with the 2002 acquisition of PriceWaterhouse Coopers Consulting. These acquisitions, along with ongoing structural changes, have significantly changed IBM's revenue model. When customers buy from IBM today, they rarely pick from an a la carte menu. Instead, they buy solutions that integrate hardware, software, and services. Increasingly, they buy these solutions not as a single transaction, but as a long-term service annuity instead. This shields IBM from the capital spending cutbacks that tend to occur when markets turn sour.

As a result of the changes the company made, IBM now attracts a greater share of customers' wallets than ever before, especially in the high-margin markets where IBM has made strategic investments. This is precisely what the company had hoped when it decided to drop lower-margin businesses that company leaders believed would not help create sales synergy going forward.

What Disney and IBM make look easy, however, is in reality very difficult. Even if a company is smart enough or lucky enough to develop multiple business models, the challenge of managing them is daunting. Technology evolutions make this difficult, as do changes in market conditions, customer buying habits, regulatory environments, and even political administrations. New business models often mean embracing new governance models, funding constructs, resource challenges, logistical obstacles, and more. Most companies, even successful ones, lack either the courage or the discipline to manage multiple business models or just shy away from the effort required due to concerns over focus and resources. They are loathe to divert resources from their primary revenue stream or to risk cannibalizing it. They are especially unlikely to make changes during the good economic times that afford them the greatest flexibility and freedom.

What most companies fail to recognize is that the inability to simultaneously pursue new and existing business models inhibits an organization from developing capabilities that it might need in the future both to exploit new opportunities and to defend itself against competitive threats. While companies like IBM and Google develop new business models to diversify their operations, others, including Amazon, have used business models to disrupt mature markets. Because brick and mortar book retailers were slow to adapt to online business models, Amazon was able to exploit the online model and thus take market share from Barnes and Noble, Borders, and others.

As Amazon and others have demonstrated, companies that do successfully embrace new business models can make significant gains that can radically change their competitiveness. Take Apple, for instance. From its founding in 1976, Apple's core business was hardware manufacturing and software development. Its products changed dramatically over the course of the company's first 25 years, but its fundamental business model did not. Apple made computer products and sold them through retailers, dealers, and mail order houses to customers around the world.

Then in the early years of the new millennium, Apple made a series of moves that would ultimately change the mix of its business models. To create a more consistent end-to-end customer buying experience, Apple opened its first retail stores in 2001. Then it introduced a disruptive technology, the revolutionary iPod music player, in October of 2001. Apple followed the launch of the iPod with a new business model that would change its trajectory even more dramatically. That was the Apple iTunes digital music store.

At the time, music downloads over the Internet were on shaky ground. Napster, a brash early innovator, was facing mounting legal challenges, while alternative models were floundering. Apple, however, believed that legal downloads of music, movies, and television programs would revolutionize the entertainment experience. And it seemed to have perfected a winning formula. Apple first secured participation from virtually every major record label. Then it created a visually appealing virtual storefront on which it showcased all but a handful of the most well-known artists in the business. Finally, it made music available one song at a time, all for the universal price of $0.99.

The combination of an elegant, innovative music player combined with an intuitive, convenient online store provided a new revenue stream that literally changed the company's fortunes. Since developing the new business model, Apple has sold more than six billion songs and millions of movies and television shows. The company now sells more music than any other retailer. iTunes is a $3 billion revenue stream that also fuels the sale of iPods. In fact, Apple now generates more revenue from its iPod product line than it amassed in total sales as a company during the year prior to the October 2001 iPod launch.[3] The impact on the company as a whole has been nothing short of revolutionary. Total sales today are now almost seven times what they were in 2001. The company's market capitalization, not surprisingly, has increased by more than 400 percent in just five years.[4] If ever there were a showcase example of the transformative powers of a new business model, Apple could be it.

And so could Cisco, if all goes according to plan.

Like Apple, Cisco has benefited handsomely from its embrace of new business models. But it hasn't been easy. Cisco's primary business model—high-value, high-margin networking products sold with partners via high-touch sales engagements—doesn't always transfer well to adjacent markets. In addition to new margin structures, Cisco has had to master different go-to-market strategies, new competitors and higher-profile branding challenges, among other things. As you might suspect, some efforts have turned out better than others. That's a polite way of saying some things tanked. But over the course of several attempts, Cisco has learned the value that can be created by pursuing both new and existing business models, and then leveraging the best from both the way Apple has done so successfully with its Macintosh computers, iPod music players, iPhone devices, and iTunes music service.

Like BYD, Cisco is constantly on the lookout for market transitions and their associated opportunities. When it spots an opportunity that fits into its overall vision, the company will pursue it regardless of whether its existing business model supports it. If the opportunity requires the adoption of a new way of doing business, Cisco will not back off. It will either develop the model required to make the most of a market transition or acquire it from a company that already has.

To Cisco, the challenges associated with developing a new business model are small compared to the loss of missing out on an important market transition.

In the pages that follow, I examine how Cisco developed new business models around opportunities such as the consumer market, custom-built video solutions, services, and collaboration software sold not as a product, but as a service. The knowledge collected from these experiences has launched the company on a new trajectory and given it the assurance that sitting idly by while markets churn or technologies change is rarely the right decision. Difficult though it may be, mustering the will to try something new, even when it threatens an existing line of revenue, has served Cisco well. Consider its expansion into consumer products, for example.

Volume Operations: A Business Model for the Consumer Market

Cisco CEO John Chambers tells a funny story about how he first came to understand the nuances of the consumer market. That's shortly after his son installed a wireless network in the family's home. "I assume you used Cisco products," said Chambers. But his son said he didn't because he couldn't find Cisco products at the retail location where he shopped. Nor could he find ones at a suitable price point online. Cisco's gear was simply too expensive and too technically advanced for his needs.

Chambers made a mental note about his son's experience. When he started asking his lieutenants if it was an isolated case, he was chagrinned by their response. "No," he was told, again and again.

That didn't sit well with the CEO, who saw huge potential in the consumer segment. At the time, the market for home and small office network connectivity products was already a $20 billion market opportunity and forecasted to grow as large as a $74 billion opportunity by 2009.[5] There was simply no way Chambers could allow Cisco to bypass that market. If consumers by the millions were networking their living spaces with inexpensive, easy-to-use routers, then Cisco ought to be at the center of this communications revolution, he believed.

But Cisco wasn't, and the reason was fairly obvious: The company's products were simply too expensive or too complex for most consumers. This wasn't due to poor pricing policies or inept engineering, but the company's vaunted business model, which produced as much wealth as all but a handful of companies in the twentieth century. To this day, Cisco's core business model relies on specific financial underpinnings without which the business cannot thrive. Cisco, for example, has traditionally aimed to achieve gross margins of 65 percent. But lower prices and steep competition makes that impossible in the consumer space, where margins of 30 percent or less are common.

What this means is that companies who compete in the consumer market have to accept some steep compromises. They cannot afford to plough 10–20 percent of revenue back into R&D. After paying distribution, branding, and other costs, consumer products manufacturers typically have around 2–3 percent of revenue left for R&D investment. Likewise, the economics of the consumer market all but eliminate the ability to offer generous customer support or flexible returns policies.

As a result, Cisco was stymied every time it tried to expand into the consumer market with its existing business model. But the market was too big and compelling to pass up. In addition to the incremental sales that could be won in the consumer space, the market offered Cisco an opportunity to increase its relevance with customers and industry watchers alike. Consider: In most markets, Cisco sold products that were largely invisible to all but a few networking professionals and technology enthusiasts. But the consumer market offered Cisco an opportunity to sell end-user devices or endpoints that customers could see and touch for themselves.

If Cisco could cement itself as the provider of networking devices for major service providers and the maker of endpoints sold to consumers, it could achieve a level of architectural influence that no other company enjoyed. But attaining that value proposition wouldn't come easy.

After several attempts to make a dent in the consumer market, Cisco could appreciate the differences between selling thousands of products priced as high as $500,000 to IT professionals versus selling millions of products priced around $50 to individual consumers. Try as it might, Cisco simply could not stretch its existing business model sufficiently to cover the consumer market. It needed a new, purpose-built business model expressly tailored to this growing segment. Among other things, this model needed to be independent from Cisco's core business and fully operational as soon as possible so Cisco wouldn't miss out on a great wave of customer buying. Given these realities, Cisco recognized that the right approach to creating the new business model would be to acquire it rather than to build it. This decision was based on how different the new business model was and how quickly it needed to be launched. Cisco chose to acquire the new business model from a company with a growing footprint in the market. The company it chose was Linksys, the maker of the equipment Chambers' son bought when it came time to install wireless connectivity in his home.

Founded in a garage in Irvine, California, in 1988 by the husband and wife team of Victor and Janie Tsao, Linksys was already a consumer networking powerhouse when Cisco came calling in 2003. Linksys had more than $400 million in annual revenue and employed more than 300 people.

From the onset, Cisco understood that it was getting into a very different business. Never before had it sold products in stores that offered Bubblicious chewing gum or Britney Spears CDs. To prevent the new business model from imploding, Cisco's management team kept much of Linksys independent, at least at the onset. They integrated common business functions, such as HR and finance, but preserved unique aspects of the company such as its engineering, sales, and marketing. Linksys, after all, was a market leader, and Cisco was eager to learn from its expertise.

The hands-off approach worked. Since the acquisition, Linksys has maintained or improved on its business metrics. Annual sales, for example, have doubled. Meanwhile, Linksys has also diversified its business and entered new markets. Today, a quarter of sales come from outside the United States—more than doubling the rate they were at a few years ago.

Thanks to its maniacal focus on enabling a separate business model, Cisco better understands branding, the retail channel, and the consumer market supply chain. Not surprisingly, the new business model, anchored in low gross margins and high volume sales, remains intact. And with this model, Cisco is inching closer to its vision of becoming a consumer-friendly company that sells devices, software, and services as an integrated solution. If not for its adoption of a new business model, Cisco might have missed out on this large and growing opportunity in the home networking market.

But the company soon realized that for all its accomplishment in the consumer space, plenty of other business models were yet to be developed if Cisco was going to expand its horizons even further.

Custom-Built: A Business Model for the Video Market

Not long after Cisco adopted a consumer business model, the company realized that rising interest in the Internet was pulling it into the complete opposite direction—toward the very companies providing consumers the Internet and broadcast content they so wanted. These companies are, of course, the world's leading telecommunications giants, cable television companies, and other service providers whose fortunes are increasingly linked to providing Internet connectivity, digital television, and IP communications.

Cisco already generated about a third of its sales from service providers, mostly from the sale of routers and switches that served as their networking infrastructure. But Cisco had yet to help the service providers sell video and other networking services to their customers. The reason was simple: Cisco lacked the technical expertise and the customized offerings needed to serve these companies to their satisfaction.

Unlike consumers, these customers don't buy anything off the shelf. They demand everything be customized for them because they believe their ability to create unique or differentiated experiences for their customers lies in the customized pieces of hardware gear and software applications they require.

Cisco, of course, longed to be the company that supplied these products to the communications giants. The difference between its capabilities and its desires at the time was akin to altering a suit bought off the rack versus tailoring one from scratch. Cisco was superb at the former, but it had limited experience with the latter. It needed a business model suited to custom-built solutions.

Without that capability, Cisco could get in only so deep with this set of customers. Once again, the company found itself poised to take advantage of an adjacent market opportunity but constrained by its traditional business model.

One reason Cisco leaders were so keen on developing a model that could cater to individual needs of large service providers was their growing interest in a technology that Cisco saw as key to its own future: video.

Video, of course, puts tremendous demand on communications and information networks and thus drives up the demand for the connectivity products that are the backbone of Cisco's product arsenal. Think about it: One hour of high-definition video consumes more bandwidth than a typical small company's email traffic consumes in a year.

You probably know that the number of videos uploaded to the Internet every day has been soaring at an astounding rate. Nearly 24 hours' worth of video is uploaded to YouTube every minute—four times as much as was uploaded just two years ago.[6] Not surprisingly, viewership is also rising rapidly. In April 2009, 17 billion video streams were initiated by Internet users in the United States. The total viewing time was almost 60 billion minutes or one billion hours.[7] That's roughly 6 minutes of video watched every day for every man, woman, and child in the United States.

All that consumption is straining the Internet like never before. Consider the impact on bandwidth of just one video: "The Last Lecture," a video of Carnegie Mellon University professor Randy Pausch delivering his final address to students shortly before his death in 2008. The emotional presentation became a viral sensation after it hit the Internet, and the understated, thoughtful professor became an unlikely media celebrity and bestselling author. As of this writing, "The Last Lecture" has been viewed more than 11 million times on YouTube, generating 3 petabytes of Internet traffic. The network traffic created by this single video is greater than all the traffic over the Internet before 1995. Staggering.

To manage the bandwidth required for video, voice, and data communications, Cisco knew that customers would need more than powerful routers and world-class switches; they would need a complete end-to-end digital solution for managing and distributing video.

Faced with the reality that it didn't have the video technology that service providers needed or the custom-built business model for catering to them, Cisco had to make a choice. It could either develop these skills internally at great cost and over a long period of time, or it could pursue another acquisition. That led it to Scientific Atlanta (SA), which Cisco acquired for $6.9 billion in 2005.

Founded in 1951, SA is best known for its set-top boxes, which are used by millions of cable TV subscribers. In addition to these devices, the company produces a complete line of video production and delivery tools and services, providing an end-to-end video solution for broadcasters, cable television companies, and production companies. Though its products are used by everyday citizens, SA's go-to-market model is anything but consumer-oriented. In contrast to Linksys, which sells items costing about $50 to millions of customers, SA's business is substantially more focused. Its top five customers, for example, average more than $200 million each in annual purchases. When Cisco approached SA, one single SA contract with Time-Warner was annually worth nearly as much as all of Linksys' annual sales.

Cisco had dealt with big customers before, but not in the way or scale in which SA did every day. SA operated with a level of service and a degree of customization that was unimaginable to Cisco. It often received last minute requests for product modifications. These would have strained Cisco's supply chain. But SA, which owns a custom-manufacturing facility in Juarez, Mexico, routinely accommodated these demands.

SA boasted a vertically-integrated, custom-built business model that enabled the company to custom-build virtually any set-top box. Managing that kind of operation and measuring its efficacy was completely foreign to Cisco. But SA had perfected it over the years. Among other things, SA developed an intimacy with customers that was new to Cisco. The executive team boasted deep, long-standing relationships with key customers—associations that had long since moved from the boardroom and into the realm of social interactions and personal friendships.

Given the differences between the Cisco and SA business models, it was decided to leave SA intact initially, until the leadership teams could map out a way to integrate SA in a mutually beneficial fashion. Over the course of three years, Cisco has integrated many go-to-market elements. More recently, Cisco has identified very specific cross-leverage plans. For example, Cisco has embraced SA's custom-built service provider model, integrating it throughout the company in every department from engineering to sales to services to help large scale telecommunications service providers. Cisco is also embracing some of the skills and techniques that SA uses to develop and nurture relationships with the CEOs of major service providers.

The Cisco/SA relationship has been mutually beneficial. In addition to the benefits that flowed to Cisco, many others flowed to SA. For example, Cisco enabled SA to expand into new geographies. At the time of the acquisition, SA had little penetration in global markets, due to the complexity of scaling its ultra high-touch model. Cisco, which generates more than half its business outside the United States, leveraged its existing relationships around the world to help SA break into new territories. Because of this, SA has flourished and is now engaged with key Cisco customers around the world.

And the result? SA's $2 billion business grew by more than 40 percent in the first two years after the acquisition, exceeding expectations.

By adopting volume-based and custom-built business models, Cisco positioned itself to serve the consumer and service provider markets more effectively.

By almost any measure, developing these two different business models at opposite ends of the spectrum simultaneously has paid off. One launched Cisco into the consumer market, while the other dramatically increased its penetration with telecommunications service providers.

An entirely different model allowed Cisco to begin servicing customers on an annuity basis years earlier.

Subscriptions: Monetizing Software Through Services

In the early 1990s, Cisco was a small, albeit fast-growing, company. Customers clamored for its networking products but also needed technical support, given the advanced nature of the technology. Like most companies, Cisco offered after-market service, mostly of the break/fix nature.

As time progressed, however, Cisco's technology evolved. So, too, did customers' dependence on it—if not for critical needs then certainly for day-to-day operations. As a result, customers began asking for greater assurances from Cisco. What they wanted, in essence, was greater support than Cisco previously provided. And to complicate the problem, customers increasingly wanted this support in geographies where Cisco had a limited footprint.

That posed a dilemma for Cisco. To better serve its customers, the company had to choose between building a significant worldwide services organization, and developing a new services model in conjunction with its partners. It wasn't an easy decision, given the enormous pressure top customers put on Cisco. They wanted the company to build a services business that would cater to them directly, but Cisco's partners had better access to them. After much deliberation, Cisco concluded it could best cater to customers' needs by creating a mechanism that maximized both Cisco's know-how and partners' abilities.

Knowing he couldn't let customers languish without adequate support, CEO John Chambers decided to build a services business in conjunction with partners. But while Cisco had the intellectual property and the technical expertise that customers wanted, it lacked the business model to provide it. Cisco's financial engine was built around products sold as single transactions, not around services, which were typically delivered as annuities over specific periods of time.

Unlike other tech giants, such as IBM or Hewlett Packard, Cisco did not want to build a full-scale, people-intensive business. Instead, it decided to develop a modest services arm to improve customer satisfaction and accelerate technology absorption, which was hampered because customers could not easily install and operate advanced Cisco products.

Because a services business is so different than a product business—think technical support and software updates instead of equipment flowing down an assembly line, and ongoing subscriptions instead of capital expenditures—the company had to develop new practices to make it successful. Chambers hired Doug Allred, a high-tech customer support executive, to develop a services business at Cisco.

Chambers gave Allred a series of key objectives: Take care of customers, increase technology absorption, earn high margins, and create a mechanism that will scale quickly around the world. With these requirements in mind, Allred began looking at options with a team that included Joe Pinto, Cisco's current senior vice president of technical services.

Customers, the team knew, needed technical support and software upgrades delivered in a more consistent fashion. But because they bought it in such an unpredictable way, Cisco struggled to monetize the business to the degree required to sustain it. Cisco realized that the complexity of its products meant that a software upgrade alone would not be sufficient for most customers; they would need a service contract that also covered advanced product replacement, online resources, and technical support.

So the new services team made a strategic decision. Cisco would offer partners the deal of a lifetime: Partners could sell lifetime service contracts of any value on Cisco equipment. In exchange, Cisco would charge them only a small percentage of the list price of any product for just a few years. The only requirement was that the partners build Cisco support capability and send their support engineers for advanced Cisco certification training. Otherwise, the terms were remarkably attractive and thousands of partners decided to create services businesses around Cisco's products.

In return, Cisco got support coverage for its customers and a predictable revenue flow to sustain the business.

With the services business monetized to the point where it was stable and predictable, Cisco began investing in best practices and other benefits for customers. Among other things, Pinto decided to publish a list of all known technical glitches or "bugs" found in Cisco products. This was unprecedented among technology companies, which have a long history of downplaying or even denying the existence of bugs in their products. While the candor surprised many in the industry, the decision to publish the list for customers' benefit ultimately won the company a great deal of goodwill among customers and helped reduce concerns they had about signing service contracts.

"Our transparency with our customers became a cornerstone of our support success," says Pinto. "It was really transformative."

So was the impact of services. By embracing a new business model, Cisco could better serve customers and help its business partners improve the profitability of their businesses. Cisco also drove growth by removing barriers to technology absorption, while adding a high-margin, annuity-based revenue stream.

One reason for the consistently high margins: Cisco promotes a self-help approach to support, leveraging its own technology. As a result, more than 80 percent of all Cisco support issues are resolved online, versus the industry average of 29 percent. By throwing intellectual property, rather than people, at the problem, Cisco improves its customer satisfaction, scales its engineering resources, and amplifies its gross margins. These high margins enable the company to reinvest in even more intellectual property, perpetuating a cycle of innovation. The business model has also grown from reactive, to responsive, to proactive, adding capabilities along the way. And the journey continues to this day, as services becomes more knowledge-centric under the leadership of Senior Vice President Gary Moore.

The new business model and the subsequent refinements worked. Services turned into a robust success for Cisco. Its gross margins exceed 65 percent—twice the industry norm—and it accounts for $7 billion in annual revenue, or one-fifth of the company's overall sales. In fiscal year 2008, Cisco services revenue grew at an annual rate of 18 percent—outpacing the growth of several of Cisco's best selling products.

Moreover, the move into services gave Cisco great confidence that it could indeed prosper with a subscription model every bit as much a traditional product sales model. The knowledge and self-assuredness Cisco developed in services came in handy when another market transition occurred in software. That was the shift from license sales to Software as a Service (SaaS). When this happened, it presented a golden opportunity for Cisco to take advantage of its experience with a subscription model to build a leadership position in collaboration.

Software as a Service: A New Way to Engage Customers

In the world of automobile manufacturing, few things excite customers more than the arrival of a new vehicle. It can prick up the ears of drivers thinking about a trade-in and attract attention from enthusiasts looking for something shiny and new.

When Subaru of America debuted the Tribeca in 2006, the company attracted more than the usual amount of attention. Its new vehicle, an upscale sports utility vehicle, was the company's first foray into the luxury car segment and came out at a time when sales were soaring in the United States.

To prepare dealers for a new category of customers, Subaru wanted to train its salespeople. But Darryl Draper, Subaru's national customer relations and loyalty training manager, worried that she could not reach all of the company's dealers before the new vehicle arrived in showrooms. After considering her options, she decided to deviate from her tried and true training method, which revolved around physically visiting every dealer. For the Tribeca, she would use the Internet.

It was a radical but theoretically feasible option given the rise of a new type of technology: web conferencing and collaboration software. Draper selected an application, developed content, and launched Subaru's training program. Within six months, she connected with 98 percent of the company's dealers and did so for a fraction of what she normally spent on training. Thanks to the collaboration software, Draper reduced training costs per person to just $0.75 per salesperson. "No other program in Subaru's history has achieved these types of results," she said.[8] With results like that, it's no wonder that collaboration is a hot category in software. More than a mere training vehicle, web conferencing and collaboration software enable an entirely new way to communicate, share information, and engage people. Among other things, it enables geographically dispersed people to host meetings with one another and jointly work together over the Internet. They can use it to share documents, host video conferencing calls with multiple participants, and deliver presentations for an almost unlimited audience. The software is a tremendous productivity tool that can reduce the distance between people and the time that separates them.

As you might imagine, sales are soaring. In 2008, worldwide sales of web conference and team collaboration software jumped 22 percent over 2007 to nearly $2 billion.[9] In an otherwise down economy, that's very strong growth.

The more Cisco looked at collaboration, the more it believed it held the promise to transform business. That's why it wanted a piece of that fast-growing market. However, Cisco was stymied by the way in which customers were consuming web conference and collaboration software. Rather than buying it outright in the traditional, software-licensing sense, customers were opting to pay for it as a subscription, otherwise known as Software as a Service (SaaS).

SaaS, much to the chagrin of traditional software companies, has been growing in popularity in the past five years. One of its earliest proponents, Salesforce.com, is already a $1 billion powerhouse in the world of business applications.

SaaS provides customers a more flexible and scalable way to pay for the software they use. For starters, customers don't generally need to install additional hardware or software in their infrastructure in order to use SaaS. Instead, they only need to be online to avail themselves of services that essentially live on the Internet, also known as the networking cloud. Among the benefits of this model is the reduced time required for customers to get up and running. Unlike traditional software applications, which can take weeks, months, and even years to roll out in a large enterprise, SaaS applications can be turned on almost instantly. SaaS is also easier on customers' wallets. It typically draws from a company's operating budget instead of its capital outlay, so signing up for SaaS doesn't require committing to a large, upfront expenditure. Because of this, customers can more easily match their spending to their needs.

SaaS also provides many benefits to software companies. Rather than sell their intellectual property as a product license in a one-time transaction, software developers can offer their work in a more flexible fashion, tailoring pricing plans to the individual needs of their customers. As a result, they can count on revenue to pour in over a measured period of time, rather than in unpredictable spurts followed by periods of drought. That's made the business of developing code less of a mad-dash and more of a deliberate run at a sustainable pace.

Cisco felt an urgency to enter the new space, given the eagerness of customers to buy and the onslaught of potential competitors. But the company was a newcomer to SaaS, which had rhythms and nuances all its own. The market, while adjacent to Cisco's existing areas of expertise, was different. It required an entirely new business model.

Cisco would need to become, in essence, a service provider, to host the applications associated with SaaS. That meant developing massive backend infrastructure and operating large data centers in order to provide subscription-based services for a monthly fee. Cisco would even need to compete with some of its own service provider customers. And for a company accustomed to dealing in large capital expenditures, the subscription-based services represented a major change to Cisco's selling model. Faced with these challenges, Cisco again looked outside its own walls for an existing business that could help launch it quickly into this market. It found what it was looking for in WebEx, which it acquired for $3.2 billion in 2007.

WebEx not only offered Cisco a hot new technology in a category for which it had great affinity, but it also provided an excellent opportunity for Cisco to make inroads in the small business market. This market had always viewed Cisco as a desirable, albeit expensive, supplier of networking gear for corporate customers. With WebEx and its small business-friendly SaaS model, Cisco had the opportunity to engage millions of potential new customers—including Subaru dealerships, which leveraged WebEx for its successful online training program.

Since the acquisition, Cisco has learned volumes about software pricing, upgrade cycles, and even new sales techniques related to the SaaS way of doing business. With a better understanding of the SaaS market under its belt, Cisco has worked to integrate WebEx into its broader go-to-market strategy. Cisco partners are now being recruited to support the WebEx platform and introduce it into their accounts, while Cisco's salespeople are incented to offer the technology to enterprise customers.

Before WebEx, Cisco simply didn't have the proper knowledge of billing practices, sales techniques, or development procedures required for this type of business. Nor did it have a way to help customers accommodate broad IT changes. "From a technological standpoint, Cisco clearly saw where the market was going in terms of cloud computing and SaaS. But that was only half of what it takes to be a leader in this market," says WebEx co-founder and Cisco vice president Subrah Iyar. "The other part of the challenge is developing the underlying business model that will allow a company to take its products and services to market in a way that customers want to consume it. Through WebEx, Cisco quickly got the technology it wanted and the business model that it needed to be a leader in this market."

While more challenges remain, the new model is working well so far—so much that WebEx net product bookings grew more than 40 percent in the first year after the acquisition.

Model Behavior

By once again doing both—pursuing new and existing business models alike—Cisco has positioned itself to be as nimble as it is strong and as flexible as it is precise. That helps when market transitions occur and every other day of the year, too.

Many companies resist new business models, fearing the inherent risks associated with them. And it's true that Cisco won't implement just any model. But if a business model has the potential to help Cisco capture a market transition or better serve its customers, then the company is quick to embrace it, whether by organic development or external acquisition. And Cisco has, by trial and error, developed best practices for each.

Of course, Cisco's efforts remain a work in progress. But the results to date are compelling. Because it embraced new and unfamiliar business models, Cisco is making inroads in previously inaccessible markets. In 2009, for example, Cisco generated $7 billion from services, $3.5 billion from video, and is approaching $1 billion each from the consumer market and from collaboration sold as a service. That's almost one-third of the company's sales—an impossibility without the embrace of a new way of doing business.

Such diversity, of course, has made Cisco a stronger company with a wider customer base and a deeper product portfolio. This is providing Cisco the kind of financial strength and resilience that used to be the stuff of fiction.

But getting to this point required some heavy lifting and some new thinking by company leaders (Table 3.1). They had to open their minds to developing capabilities in disciplines they had never before mastered.

TABLE 3.1 Summary of New Business Models

Market Opportunity	Business Model	Offering	Method of Market Entry	Go-to-Market Strategy
Consumer	Volume operations	Home networking	Acquisition	Retail
Video	Custom-built solutions	Networked video	Acquisition	Direct
Services	Subscription	Customer support	Internal development	Partners
Collaboration	Software as a Service	Web collaboration	Acquisition	Online

Think about that the first time a silent, emission-free, electric car from China zooms past you in a flash of metal and chrome. In your rush to seize a photo of that technological marvel with your mobile phone, remember that BYD built that car on the profits it made from the battery inside that phone. Like Cisco, it was willing to step outside its comfort zone to embrace a new business model.

In doing so, it may change the world.

4

Tuning *and* Transforming
Optimization and Reinvention

Two billion dollars.

That's how much value was lost in one of the costliest supply-chain snafus in business history. The company behind the mess: Cisco. That's right, *we* were responsible for one of the biggest fiascos in the history of manufacturing and logistics. Eight years later, it still serves as a powerful lesson worth studying. Here's why.

In the annals of "supply chain disasters"—yes, there are accounts of such things—several business mishaps stand out. There's the 1999 Hershey Foods meltdown that occurred after a new warehouse and inventory management system went awry. It thwarted Hershey from delivering Halloween candy on time and cost the chocolate giant more than $150 million in lost revenue. There's also the Aris Isotoner glove snafu of 1994, which led to a 50 percent drop in sales after the company switched factories in an ill-fated attempt to save on production costs.[1]

Each of these mistakes offers lessons in what to do and what not to do when it comes to implementing and organizing your supply chain. But the Cisco debacle of 2001 is hard to top when it comes to illustrating the cost of an operational nightmare. Cisco's blunder cost it a staggering sum of money. But at least the company could address its shortcomings. Others haven't been so lucky.

Take the famed German fashion house Escada, for example, which has dressed some of Europe's most wealthy women and Hollywood's most fashionable stars since its founding in 1976. In recent years, the likes of actresses Katherine Heigl and Oscar-winner Hilary Swank have been seen wearing Escada at red carpet events.

Known for its aggressive styles, trademark animal prints and exquisite embroidery work, Escada established itself as a fashion trendsetter in the 1980s. Then in the 1990s, the company pioneered "seasonal fragrances" for women. With the help of acquisitions, it also expanded into eyewear, shoes, jewelry, scarves, and neckwear.[2]

Despite Escada's hefty prices, the company charmed critics with its unique mix of fabrics and colors and built a devoted following among savvy, upwardly mobile shoppers. Season after season, it dressed celebrities, garnered magazine covers, and grew its fan base. At its zenith, the Munich-based company boasted thousands of employees, hundreds of boutiques, and more than 500,000 customers worldwide.[3]

Despite the popularity of its alluring haute couture line, trendy sportswear, and chic fragrances, Escada struggled financially in recent years. The reason: It never could instill enough discipline in its operations. As a result, Escada spent much of the 2000s trying to get a handle on its finances after years of acquisitions, unsuccessful product launches, and ill-timed geographic expansions. Among other things, the company decided to drop beauty care products and abandon its lingerie line.[4] Then it moved to undo many of the deals that it had previously completed. At one point, it announced plans to sell its Primera division, which is responsible for its apriori, BiBA, cavita, and Laurél products.[5] Later still, Escada pulled back from opening new stores, including one in New York that had reportedly been under development for two years.[6]

No matter what it tried, Escada could not lift its operational competency anywhere near the level of its design excellence. The company could change consistently with new styles, new merchandise, and new advertising. When it expanded into categories such as jewelry, handbags, and fragrances, customers followed willingly. But it could not operationalize this grand vision, nor perfect its execution. As a result, the company's financial fortunes suffered. In 2008, Escada posted a net loss of €70 million on depressed sales that slumped 15 percent over 2007. Rather than blame the economy solely for the company's foibles, Escada's management team provided a frank summary of challenges when explaining the company's misfortunes in the 2008 company annual report: "These results are not only attributable to adverse conditions, but they are also a consequence of internal deficits in organizational processes and market operations."

Unable to optimize the basic mechanics of their business in time to save the company, Escada's leaders declared their company insolvent in August 2009. Just as Escada was about to go under in late 2009, Megha Mittal, a member of the ArcelorMittal steel family, stepped in and acquired the company, vowing to reduce its debt, restore profits, and expand sales into Asia.[7]

Escada's woes underscore how important it is for a company not to over-emphasize the reinvention of its product line at the expense of the optimization of its operations.

Other companies have experienced the express opposite.

Take Dell Computer, for example.

Few companies in history have exceeded—or even met—the level of operational excellence that Dell achieved in the 1990s and early 2000s. And it did so against notable companies like IBM, HP, and Compaq. None was a match for Dell's relentless drive for operational excellence. Year after year, Dell reduced costs, improved manufacturing efficiencies, and streamlined product delivery. That unbeatable combination proved successful for Dell, which overtook Compaq as the world's leading PC supplier in 2001.[8] Throughout the early part of the decade, rivals and onlookers alike lamented and marveled at how Dell could set the pace for the industry.

In 2005, *Fortune* magazine placed Dell at the top of its "Most Admired Companies" list. But the March 7, 2005, issue hinted at the troubles that would soon haunt the company: "Dell's peers see it as a brilliantly managed brand—but no innovator in raw computing."[9]

Indeed, the computer maker from Round Rock, Texas, fell out of favor after a series of management changes, product disappointments, and market blunders.[10] The company learned a painful lesson in consumer electronics, for example, after it launched a line of portable MP3 players designed to compete with the Apple iPod. Deemed inferior by consumers, the products turned out to be market duds, and Dell pulled the plug on them in 2006. The company also had high hopes for its flat-screen TVs, which were featured on a *Fortune* magazine cover along with company founder Michael Dell. But they, too, failed to attract much in the way of customer interest. Dell discontinued them in 2007.

Dell's inability to reinvent itself, especially on the product front, soon led to other humbling setbacks, including the departure of then-CEO Kevin Rollins and the failure to meet earnings projections for several quarters.[11]

Suddenly the one-time operations giant looked flustered. Experts began looking beyond the company's operations and instead pointed their fingers at its inventiveness. At the time of Rollins' 2007 exit, for example, many of Dell's top managers were business experts or management gurus, not technologists. That, in addition to management priorities and company strategy, may explain why Dell's innovation slipped behind that of HP and others, who typically plough 3 percent or more of revenue into research and development—triple what Dell invests.[12]

The billions of dollars that HP, for example, invested translated into a significant edge once the PC market bifurcated in the middle of the decade. Up to that point, Dell's aggressive prices and product quality seemed to hit squarely in the sweet spot of customer demands. But then customer buying patterns shifted. Customers wanted either high-end devices packed with new features and plenty of innovation or bare-bones products stripped of frills but capable of running businesses and consumer households just the same. Dell found itself caught in the middle of this market evolution, unable to match the inventiveness of Apple, the operational execution of HP, or the aggressive prices of Asian manufacturers.

A 2008 article in *Forbes* magazine zeroed in on Dell's situation, pinpointing why the company was adrift: "Dell is missing the biggest element in the turnaround at Apple: deep product design teams. Both Apple and HP appealed to consumers to claw their way out of slumps. Apple, under Chief Executive Steve Jobs, launched catchy new products ranging from all-in-one iMacs to the iPod line of digital music players. Hewlett-Packard, likewise, poured resources into designing slick, retail-friendly PCs to compete on crowded store shelves even as it was slashing jobs and shuttering excess manufacturing capacity. That was good enough to move HP past Dell to the top spot in the PC business."[13]

The stories of Escada and Dell illustrate what can happen when a company emphasizes either optimization or reinvention to the exclusion of the other. Escada's over-reliance on creativity brought the company to its knees. Dell's obsession with operational excellence, meanwhile, prevented the company from delivering innovations that the market wanted, costing it a great deal of goodwill and prestige. When *Fortune* announced its list of "Most Admired Companies" in 2009, Dell, the leader from just four years prior, wasn't even mentioned in the top 50.[14]

With the return of founder and CEO Michael Dell, Dell is attempting to remedy its past mistakes with a renewed focus on innovation. Likewise, Mittal is trying to optimize financial and operational discipline at Escada.

Over the years, Cisco, too, has struggled with doing both tuning and transforming simultaneously. Its own supply chain debacle epitomizes what can happen when a company prioritizes one discipline over another.

Could a company that endured one of the worst supply chain debacles in business history realistically become one of the best practitioners in business? In the years that followed the $2 billion write-off, Cisco set out in search of the answer. To do so, it would have to optimize *and* reinvent. Tune and transform. At the same time.

Waking Up to the New Reality

If your company manufactures something or relies on partners that do, chances are you're already familiar with a supply chain. For the uninitiated, supply chain is the term used to describe the design and development of products and solutions and the combination of companies, facilities, and processes required for building and moving a good or service from a point of production to an end user. The more complicated the product, the more complex the supply chain required. High-tech goods, which often include microchips, circuit boards, disk drives, power supplies, and other components too numerous to mention, require very sophisticated supply chains. That's certainly true of the products Cisco develops.

Today, Cisco's supply chain team oversees more than 300 product families, representing 23,500 products, including high-end switches, mid-range networking products, IP phones, routers, and set-top cable TV boxes. Cisco custom-configures most of these products through a series of regional logistics hubs and ships them to virtually every country on earth from facilities located on three continents. Most products are built to order, and most get delivered to a customer without any Cisco employee ever touching them.

As capable as it is today, Cisco's supply chain wasn't always so accomplished. In fact, there was a time that it almost upended the company. The aforementioned calamity took place in the aftermath of the 2001 dot-com collapse. To understand it fully, you must first think about the dot-com boom. In the late 1990s, dot-com companies were forming almost overnight in what can only be described as a gold rush. Business plans thrown together in a matter of weeks or even days attracted funding from venture capitalists, who advised their clients to spend whatever they needed on branding and equipment to establish themselves on the Internet as fast as possible.

That, of course, played right into Cisco's hands. At the peak of the boom, Cisco was the supplier of choice for Internet gear and expertise. In 2000, for example, sales jumped 55 percent to $19 billion. That was good enough to lift the company to number 107 on the *Fortune 500* list from number 146 in the previous year. And Wall Street rewarded Cisco handsomely by driving its stock to record heights. In October of 1998, a Cisco share traded for $15.75. By March 2000, it was trading at more than $80.

With success, however, came new challenges. In 1999, the company was struggling to make equipment fast enough to keep up with demand. The time between orders and delivery (lead time) on the company's hot-selling Catalyst 6000 Series stretched out to three months at one point—an eternity for startups desperate to get their businesses up and running. Many companies resorted to placing double and triple orders with the hopes that one of their requests would come through on time. That only exacerbated Cisco's supply challenges.

Inside the company, for example, product groups began to compete against one another for third-party components. T.S. Khurana, Cisco's director of global supply chain management, remembers groups of employees actually arguing over shipments of much-needed tantalum capacitors (a device that helps manage electricity inside sophisticated electronic equipment). "We were at competition with each other and with the cell phone market over individual piece parts," says Khurana. "It was a crazy time."

Faced with a growing demand problem, Cisco leaders considered building more factories. But they knew the company's core differentiation lay elsewhere—not in the realm of manufacturing, but in product innovation and customer relationships. So they began to overhaul the company's supply chain capabilities. For starters, Cisco began outsourcing more of its manufacturing to third-party vendors. Then it began to connect their different IT systems and business operations with Cisco's own enterprise resource planning (ERP) system and data standards. Finally, in an attempt to manage production costs and to prevent piracy and gray marketing, Cisco took control of the inventory that its third-party partners produced. The company essentially embraced a consignment model.

While all these creative moves helped Cisco regain some control over its supply chain, they left the company in a vulnerable position. That was especially true of the decision to embrace the consignment model. What if the market ever turns sour, some wondered? Would it find itself with a lot of product on its books?

In theory, yes. But few at the time thought Cisco would ever find itself in such a position. Then, of course, the unthinkable happened: The bubble burst.

The euphoria investors had for backing companies promising to sell pet supplies, groceries, and toys over the Internet evaporated. When this happened, the Cisco customers who had placed multiple orders at the height of the frenzy disappeared overnight. As a result, Cisco's sales trajectory did a 180-degree turn. In less than 100 days, Cisco's year-over-year growth-rate went from 66 percent positive to 45 percent negative.

Despite the slowdown in demand, Cisco's contract manufacturing plants kept churning out products. They did so to catch up with the backlog of orders, thinking the downturn was a momentary pause. Unfortunately, many of those orders, the company soon learned, were either desperate attempts to overcome allocation backlogs or wishful dreams placed by companies that soon found themselves with no means to pay. Regardless, Cisco quickly found itself with billions of dollars worth of routers, switches, and other gear that no one wanted. Worse yet, much of it was custom-configured for companies that had gone out of business or were in serious financial jeopardy. The bottom line: There was no way Cisco could sell a sizable percent of its excess inventory within six months, so, the company had to do the unthinkable: scrap the products for parts. In the end, Cisco wrote off more than $2 billion in inventory.

At the time, company watchers were anything but kind to Cisco, a company they believed had come to epitomize the high-tech manufacturer that rode the dot-com market exuberance to unsustainable heights. When the collapse occurred, more than a few were glad to see Cisco tumble from its lofty perch. In an article posted on the industry news site CNET in 2001, market watcher and financial analyst Tad LaFountain from Needham & Co. said, "As a result of what has transpired, network equipment management might consider looking beyond the car in front of them as they speed down the information superhighway."[15]

Since 2001, Cisco has been the subject of innumerable post-mortems about the dot-com phenomenon. Most experts understand how Cisco got caught up in the euphoric atmosphere that resulted from runaway sales growth and unprecedented market capitalization appreciation. But the inventory write-off remains another story. How could the company have built so much unwanted product, supply chain experts wonder? Many at Cisco have asked no less.

Though several factors contributed to the problem, the underlying issue was fairly simple: In an attempt to keep up with demand, Cisco reinvented at the expense of optimization. As a result, the company became blind to flaws that would eventually contribute to the setback it sustained.

Cisco had developed a very capable supply chain in the late 1990s. But it was originally built to do one thing: keep up with demand. At the time, demand was so great that Cisco, in some instances, chartered private aircraft to transport goods to customers. It also provided working capital to component manufacturers, who could then get established quickly and start supplying much-needed products to Cisco. That kind of entrepreneurial zeal and process innovation propelled the company when the market was zooming, but not after it began to freefall.

In the end, Cisco was upended by a dramatic reversal in market demand, which was further exacerbated by additional failings. Among other things, the company failed to factor into its forecasts the double and triple orders customers placed in the hopes of avoiding delayed shipments. That deluded the company into thinking that it should gear up for annual growth rates of more than 40 percent. Cisco also invested too much faith in the promise of the new Internet economy, which did not ultimately nullify the need for good, old-fashioned operational excellence. Finally, Cisco should have anticipated that its consignment inventory model would be problematic in an economic downturn. But it did not.

So how did this happen? Amid the dot-com euphoria, Cisco leaders forgot that boom times are typically followed by busts. Experience may also have played a factor. The company had a young, albeit energetic, manufacturing team. But who could blame them for their unbridled optimism? With so many outsiders heaping praise on the company, Cisco leaders didn't see much reason to change their practices or believe that the days of unrestricted growth would come to an end anytime soon. But that optimism blinded them to the fact that their supply chain, which was designed around a few basic product lines, lacked flexibility. As the company's product portfolio expanded, Cisco needed a supply chain that could accommodate everything from high-volume consumer products to one-off, specialized products for very large institutional buyers. In the early part of the 2000s,

Cisco's supply chain was simply not built to handle this type of complexity because the company failed to plan for anything but growth.

Fixing the problem, however, would require significant effort. One reason: complexity. Cisco found itself with a mix of internal organizational silos, external manufacturing partners, and third-party logistics specialists. The company recognized that it would need to coordinate the activities of different business units and entities, disparate technologies, and multiple time zones. Short of this, Cisco knew it could not take advantage of market transitions or prepare for shifting economic conditions the way that companies with world-class supply chains could. At these organizations, supply chain management has evolved from a back-office specialty into a boardroom priority. In fact, many of the most successful companies in today's global, interconnected marketplace are focusing on supply chain management as a source of competitive advantage.

Despite—or perhaps because of—its past problems, Cisco decided to prioritize its supply chain management. To that end, the company has invested millions of dollars in its supply chain operations, especially in the areas of logistics, technology, and training. But fixing a supply chain requires more than money, the company has learned. Changes in business processes and culture in particular also figure into the equation.

The steps Cisco needed to take would have significant ramifications for the company.

Picking Up the Pieces

After the write-off, Cisco examined virtually every aspect of its supply chain. It quickly identified 45 different parts of the company that had a direct impact on manufacturing and distribution—too many. The company also discovered that more than 120 different spreadsheets were used to influence decisions pertaining to the supply chain. There were different methods for looking at key metrics such as bookings, backlogs, and inventory. And nearly every organization in the company used its own automation tool. These tools were supposed to work together but often didn't because they were built during a bygone era—an era when business units, flush with cash, invested in their own tools, with little concern for other departments.

Khurana describes the way that the pre-recession mentality was impacting the company after the bubble burst. "Before the dot-com crash, budgets meant nothing," he says. "You had a budget but knew you could blow past it because your sales growth would cover any overage. At that time, you could do things like ask IT to build you a specific tool to support your growth. And in the environment of the day, that was ok because it supported growth. It seemed like a perfect system until the bottom fell out of the market."

Cisco's supply chain operations improved sharply when the company began to optimize. That included overhauling its organizational structure, rationalizing its partnering strategy, and streamlining its product inventory. The changes impacted everything from tools to business models to operational procedures. Suddenly inventory turns mattered a lot more. So did returns on investments and product quality, as well as lead times and life cycles.

After a concerted effort, the company rationalized its parts inventory and eliminated literally thousands of SKUs. It also reduced the number of component companies and third-party manufacturers it worked with and rededicated itself to getting close to a smaller number of partners. Instead of negotiating with more than 1,300 component suppliers, for example, Cisco instituted a Preferred Supplier Program that took the number down to less than 300 in just four years. It also reduced the number of contract manufacturers that it worked with from 20 to 4.

Then Cisco worked to equip its suppliers with the latest in electronic tools and processes to gain visibility throughout its entire supply chain. It began working closely with suppliers to share best practices and implement consistent processes. Afterward, Cisco reassessed its own technological capabilities. Instead of spreadsheets and email messages, the company implemented a state-of-the-art manufacturing system to drive alignment between, and improve forecasting accuracy across, various business units, sales teams, and manufacturing organizations.

Cisco also changed its organizational structure. Take the company's "master schedulers," for example—the people responsible for day-to-day output of products and for long-term inventory planning. Given the nature of their jobs, master schedulers rarely had an opportunity to consider the long-term outlook of the supply chain. To address this, the company divided the role into two distinct jobs: long-term planner and short-term specialist. With dedicated long-term planners in place, Cisco could better plan for changing buying patterns and business conditions.

More than mere process or technology changes, the work Cisco undertook between 2000 and 2005 represented a significant cultural shift for Cisco and marked the end of the company's "cowboy" days.

No longer whiz kids who could conceal operational inefficiencies with record sales, Cisco supply chain managers saw their shortcomings—in real time. They had to pull together as a team.

As a result, business metrics began to improve. Inventory turns, for example, increased by more than 50 percent between 2001 and 2005. Finally, Cisco improved on its forecasting accuracy.

By then, however, these optimization efforts started to generate diminishing returns. Inventory turns, which had increased by 50 percent, flattened. Improvements in key metrics continued, but changes were incremental, not transformative. Cisco realized that optimization, while necessary, wasn't sufficient. It also needed to reinvent.

"We were better, but we didn't really know what we wanted to be," says Khurana.

The answer to that dilemma would come from a new leader who energized the manufacturing team by focusing it, once again, on reinvention. Only this time, the company was keen on not doing it at the expense of optimization.

From Tuning to Transforming

Enter Angel Mendez, Cisco's senior vice president of Global Supply Chain Management.

As a young man, Mendez studied to become an engineer. But when he got a summer job working at GE in one of its manufacturing facilities, he became hooked on operations and logistics. After a successful stint at GE, Mendez moved on to Allied Signal, Citibank, and Palm Computing, helping to lift operational performance at every step.

"Once a factory guy, always a factory guy," he says.

When he joined Cisco in 2005, the deficiencies and weaknesses that had led to the 2001 problems were largely a thing of the past. Cisco had strong operational processes and greater flexibility. But Mendez, nonetheless, saw room for improvement. More than anything, he worried that the company's supply chain wasn't structured to keep pace with global growth or to respond to rapidly changing customer needs. He also worried about overall cohesiveness; while individual groups made improvements, there was no focus on overall team improvement.

His efforts would transform Cisco's supply chain once more.

Shortly after taking over the helm of Cisco's manufacturing arm, Mendez and his leadership team recognized that the transformation Cisco needed would require a more unified, holistic approach to the many different capabilities that comprised the company's supply chain operations—from forecasting and demand planning through manufacturing, quality management, delivery, and product reuse and recycling. So he quickly mobilized his team. After some analysis, the team realized that the Cisco supply chain was optimized for a bygone era. The team feared that if it didn't move quickly, Cisco could miss out on the next major wave of change in the IT and telecommunications marketplace.

Cisco's supply chain, they reckoned, was set up to handle upgrades and enhancements to existing product lines and to make it easy for partners to engage with Cisco. What the supply chain wasn't prepared to do was configure and deliver solutions that met exacting customer needs, including the unique requirements of diverse global markets. The supply chain was also not ready to take on new, disruptive innovations that could change the way businesses bought, deployed, and used technology. Considering that these were the very areas that Cisco was pursuing, this was a significant problem. For Mendez and his boss, Executive Vice President Randy Pond, the situation called for change.

It was time to reinvent.

One of their first decisions was to evolve Cisco from a supply-push model to a demand-pull model. In simple terms, that meant no longer building products based on dreams or expectations, but instead on actual customer orders. Because it frees manufacturers from filling their warehouses with goods that may never sell, the demand-pull model is more efficient and less risky than its predecessor. But it does require a high level of systems responsiveness.

Cisco did not have the necessary systems then. But Mendez was determined that it soon would. To get a better understanding of what was needed, his team studied 30 leading manufacturers from technology, consumer products, and even pharmaceuticals. In particular, Cisco benchmarked the perceived supply chain management leaders, including Dell, Walmart, and Procter & Gamble. These companies handled sophisticated products, global suppliers, and changing technology. They could also forecast effectively, address changing supply costs efficiently, and tailor deliverables to customer needs quickly. Why not Cisco, Mendez wondered?

"I want us to set a goal to become the world leader in supply chain management in three years," he announced to his team.

That pricked up more than a few ears. After all, Cisco wasn't even an afterthought in the annual contest that mattered to manufacturing experts and operational gurus: the annual AMR Research ranking of the world's top 25 leaders in supply chain excellence—a list featuring companies like Walmart and Dell. Over the years, AMR has established a numerical index for judging excellence, which includes a combination of hard and soft metrics. Some things were straightforward: How many inventory turns did your company complete this year? What financial results did it drive? The softer points came from a poll of manufacturers, leading researchers, academics, and AMR's own research experts. To land on the AMR list, a company has to not only perform brilliantly, but also attract peer recognition. Being on the list is correlated with company performance. Companies on the AMR list, for example, have outperformed the Dow Jones and S&P 500 indices by as much as 15 percent in both up years and down.

Prior to 2005, Cisco never even earned a mention on the list. Yet Mendez had the audacity to suggest that Cisco had the will, talent, and global resources to *win* this "Miss Universe Crown" of manufacturing excellence in just three years. It was a bold goal to say the least.

To embrace a demand-pull model, achieve greater efficiencies, and win the hearts and minds of the experts at AMR, Mendez knew that his organization faced a daunting challenge. Most importantly, his top leaders would need to look beyond their immediate spheres of responsibility and work together across functions. To help focus the team's attention around a common mission, Mendez launched a new plan called Manufacturing Excellence, or Mx. This was a plan for delivering an agile, innovative, and collaborative supply chain that could translate Cisco innovation into high-quality products and scale across technologies, customer segments, geographies, and partners.

At first, some members of the team questioned the plan. Undaunted, Mendez persevered and launched the program. Shortly thereafter, nearly half of the people in his 1,900-person organization found themselves in new roles with new job descriptions. Groups doing "A"-level work within functional silos were suddenly asked to move out of their comfort zones and work more collaboratively with teams from other areas. Product and manufacturing engineers were thrust together to resolve quality issues, while demand planners had to start conversations with Cisco colleagues, suppliers, and contract manufacturers that they hardly knew. Everyone was expected to consider the bigger picture and view the supply chain as a whole. Some employees loved the change, but others, including some senior leaders, were skeptical.

"Culture and mindset, not complexity, were a large part of the challenge," says Mendez.

Some in Mendez' team equated his determination to transform as another exercise in operational efficiency. They didn't see the need to improve what they had because they weren't feeling any pain; they were fulfilling orders and making efficient use of existing systems. But they weren't seeing the value that was trapped in their ways of doing business or the opportunities just beyond their operations. Put bluntly, they saw no need for wholesale changes.

The united team, however, did. And so it pressed on with Mx, which it believed would give Cisco the flexibility and capability it needed to compete in an era where extracting efficiencies from a physical flow of goods was not as important as unleashing value for customers. That meant viewing every supply chain function—from collaborative planning to monitoring circuit yields at remote factories—as part of the same effort to drive innovation and increase relevance to customers.

To make sure that Mx took root, the leadership team tasked individuals from supply chain, sales, and engineering to address specific challenges. They were told to shed their functional hats and work collectively to solve common problems. "No one could say 'the problem is in your end of the boat.' We were all in this together," says Mendez. Another change: Job roles were no longer categorized by product, but instead by process and logistics. No longer were employees product experts; they were supply chain experts. That forced managers to collaborate more than ever before and to take responsibility for a broader set of issues. It was initially daunting to some because it represented a landmark change in just about every aspect of the organization.

In a follow-up program, launched in 2007, Cisco looked for ways to streamline inventory for distribution partners, recover value from used and returned products, and listen directly to customers. That led to the creation of a new manufacturing model, involving supply chain partners like Hon Hai Precision Industry (Foxconn), one of the world's largest contract manufacturers.

"Moving to a pull manufacturing model was very ambitious, but the right business decision," says Michael Ling, general manager of Hon Hai's Communications & Networking Solution Business Group. "On the one hand, Cisco is a tough and demanding customer. On the other hand, we work together to set challenging and rewarding goals. When we achieve the goals, there is recognition for our teams, down to the individual engineer on the floor."

Despite all the gains made, both inside and outside the company, some Cisco leaders resisted the changes. Several asked for transfers, and a few even left the company. One reason: The new organizational culture put an end to the "blame game." If there was a problem, it had to be fixed by Mendez's team. No more blaming a vendor, another Cisco department, or some outside force; if it impacted the supply chain team, it had to be fixed by the supply chain, Mendez insisted. As much as anything, the mindset and culture of the organization had to change. Employees had to accept accountability, anticipate and embrace change, and work together as a cohesive unit.

Cisco can now forecast appropriately, enabling the company to operate with just a fraction of the inventory it once carried—manufacturing inventory turns, for example, are now almost twice what they were. Furthermore, the company can more quickly respond to customer requests and deliver more reliably. In addition, the quality of the components and assembled products leaving partner factories has increased, and the entire supply chain has been enhanced to serve China, India, and many emerging countries in ways the old system simply could not support.

From Jeers to Cheers

By tuning and transforming simultaneously, Cisco realized significant gains. Today, its supply chain handles twice the volume of revenue that it did back when the dot-com bubble burst, with less than half the people.

"Cisco has stayed in front of all these changes by building a value chain that employs more than 8,000 people at 50 locations in 17 countries," says Mendez. "It would not have been possible had we not done three key things: establish a radical goal that everyone had to notice, look at our partners and systems from an end-to-end basis, and, finally, take the customer's concerns into consideration."

So how have the experts at AMR Research, who rank the world leaders in supply excellence, responded to Cisco's strategy of optimizing and reinventing simultaneously? Suffice to say that they have taken notice: Cisco first made their Top 25 list three years ago and has moved up every year since. In the latest ranking, Cisco was number five.

It's not Miss Universe yet, but it is in contention.

5

Satisfied Customers *and* Gratified Partners

Direct Touch and Leveraged Influence

"A devastating, horrible mistake."

That's how third-generation car dealer Randy Painter described U.S. automaker Chrysler's decision to sever its relationship with his family's company. After doing business together for more than 65 years, Chrysler gave Painter just three week's notice. "This doesn't happen in the U.S.," he lamented to *The Wall Street Journal*.[1]

But alas it did in 2009, and not to just Painter, but to nearly 800 of Chrysler's 3,200 other dealers, too. They were told they would be cut from the ranks of Chrysler's channel partners as part of a last-ditch effort to save the beleaguered company. As Chrysler management saw it, the company was over-distributed in the United States—a situation that caused a lot of headaches.

Among other things, this meant too many dealers recruiting too few trained mechanics and experienced salespeople. This limited the success of each individual dealer. While Toyota sold nearly 1,300 vehicles per dealer in 2008, Chrysler sold just 303.[2] And dealers struggled to distinguish themselves from one another, which led to price wars and deflated margins for all. With profits hard to come by, dealers were challenged to keep their show rooms new, their repair shops up-to-date, and their salespeople properly trained. Because of this, customer service suffered and Chrysler's image took a beating.

While in Chapter 11 bankruptcy, Chrysler terminated hundreds of dealer contracts. The company hoped that this would help improve the overall climate for selling Chrysler products. Instead, the move turned out to be a public relations nightmare as dealers dug in their heels and turned to the government and the media for relief. Rather than eliminate one problem, Chrysler found itself staring down even more.

So much for a fresh start.

Instead of emerging from bankruptcy in June 2009 with a bold, new agenda, Chrysler found itself at odds with the dealer community—the very dealer community it needed if it were to cultivate ties with new customers and restore its image with existing ones. For a company that was already struggling with product quality, this was a significant setback.

Every business knows that having satisfied customers is fundamental to long-term success. The story of Chrysler illustrates that gratified partners are just as important.

If your company relies on dealers, retailers, resellers, or any number of third parties, then you likely understand just how true this is. Without partners, many companies would simply cease to exist. That's especially true of those companies who have no direct sales models. Think book publishers, gasoline refineries, automotive manufacturers, and a myriad of other organizations that do not conduct business with end customers directly, but instead through a network of intermediaries. Among other benefits, these intermediaries provide geographic reach, market access, and subject matter expertise that companies lack in-house.

For all these benefits, partners are not without challenges. They can be difficult to manage, expensive to support, and hard to retain. No problem, however, is greater than balancing the opportunity for the profitability of partners with the satisfaction of customers. And companies must find a way to do both without compromising either.

The key to doing this is to think about profitability across an entire value chain and to develop mutually beneficial strategies that build loyalty among allies while prioritizing customer satisfaction.

If your company finds itself in a struggle with its business partners, as Chrysler did, then doing both might sound counter-intuitive, if not impossible. But it isn't. A significant number of companies, from IBM to John Deere, have built loyal, dedicated followings of partners that successfully cater to end customers' needs. IBM, for one, has maintained solid partner relationships even though its direct sales force sells many of the same IBM products to many of the same customers that its reseller partners target. How does IBM keep the peace? It avoids the abrupt policy changes, wholesale strategy shifts, and punitive or confusing restrictions that sour business relationships.

In the automobile market, there may be no better example of a company that excels at this more than Lexus. Ever since its 1989 U.S. launch, Lexus has endeavored to satisfy customers and partners both. In addition to developing some of the world's most reliable cars, Lexus has meticulously addressed some of the most difficult issues facing both customers and dealers.

Hoping to avoid the challenges that plagued U.S. brands including Chrysler, Lexus management decided to limit the number of its dealerships in the United States to 250. This ensures maximum profitability for dealers and makes it easier for Lexus management to monitor quality standards. To date, there are approximately 230 authorized Lexus dealerships in the United States compared to roughly 1,400 for fellow luxury car-maker Cadillac. Despite the disparity, Lexus outsells its American counterpart by almost 2:1.

The substantially higher sales volume per dealer translates into greater margins for Lexus dealerships. In fact, dealership broker Sheldon Sandler says Lexus dealers enjoy higher profits per vehicle than any other mass-marketed luxury car dealer. "When you and I die, we should hope to come back as Lexus dealers," he told *Forbes* magazine.[3]

Thanks to the profitability they achieve, Lexus dealers have become full partners in the manufacturer's push to provide the best customer experience possible in the car industry. Lexus dealerships have installed customer-friendly features like indoor driving ranges, gourmet food counters, and even fully-functional guest offices where working professionals can hunker down while their vehicles are being serviced. And many of those investments were offset by generous contributions from Lexus back to these dealers.[4]

These outlays, along with ongoing investments in training, tools, and other resources, have distinguished Lexus in a crowded field. In 2009, the company again achieved the highest scores in both the J.D. Power and Associates Customer Service Index Study of dealer service[5] and in the University of Michigan's American Customer Satisfaction Index study.[6]

For its ability to satisfy *both* customers *and* partners, Lexus has been handsomely rewarded in the marketplace. Today, it holds the number one position in luxury car sales in the U.S. market.

Like Lexus, Cisco maintains an unwavering focus on both customer satisfaction and partner loyalty. Today, doing both is well-engrained inside the company. But this wasn't always the case.

Going the Extra Mile

At Cisco, customers have been a part of the company's focus since day one. In fact, it's the stuff of legend inside the company.

Cisco Senior Vice President Joe Pinto, for one, recalls being jolted from a peaceful slumber one night by a phone call from a company security guard who caught a man breaking into one of Cisco's engineering labs. As fate would have it, the man was a company employee who worked for Pinto in Cisco's customer support organization. What was he doing in a locked engineering lab without authorization in the dead of night, Pinto asked? Stealing a networking card from an internal company server. The card was out of stock at the time, but the employee had promised to secure one for a customer before visiting him later that day.

"Let him go," Pinto told the security officer, "*with* the card."

From CEO John Chambers on down, Cisco has carefully and meticulously cultivated a culture that prioritizes customer interests. Take Pinto. Each quarter, he meets—and even shares his home phone number—with hundreds of customers. He often begins presentations with observations about those interactions, and personally monitors the satisfaction of customers big and small.

Pinto credits his upbringing in one of New York City's toughest neighborhoods for giving him the skills to get along with others and defuse stressful situations.

To him, soothing customers' concerns and focusing on their satisfaction just came naturally. He remembers one Easter Sunday, when he took a dozen calls at home and spent the entire holiday on the phone. "We treated customers like family and made sacrifice just a part of how we did things," he says.

That work continues to this day.

Cisco invests a significant sum into measuring customer satisfaction *on a daily basis*. The company has gone so far as to develop a real-time, customer satisfaction dashboard that is available to the entire workforce. At the mere click of a mouse, every employee can see up-to-date satisfaction numbers for every country, product, and customer segment. Walker Research, which administers these surveys for Cisco and other technology leaders, reports that Cisco's satisfaction level today hovers around 4.5 on a 5-point scale—well above the industry average.

To make sure that employees take these numbers seriously, Cisco ties their compensation directly to customer satisfaction. Today, the customer satisfaction index can influence employee bonuses by as much as 40 percent. To no one's surprise, fluctuations are among the most closely monitored business indicators inside the company.

But this customer-centric culture goes beyond mere measurements and metrics. At Cisco, there are well-defined and finely-honed best practices for virtually every conceivable type of customer interaction. Be it troubleshooting support, designing networks, or even locating spare parts when none are available through traditional channels, Cisco has developed replicable, scalable, and proven processes to help customers at every turn. And if these should somehow fail, Cisco has back-up procedures in place, too. Critical account lists are monitored by the hour, while teams of support engineers are on standby to mobilize resources instantly. When Saudi Telecom, for example, had a critical network issue, Cisco immediately dispatched one of its top U.S. support engineers to the Kingdom. The mission: do whatever it takes to satisfy the customer. For seven straight months, the engineer worked three weeks out of four in Saudi Arabia. In that time, the customer went from one of Cisco's most disappointed to one of its most loyal in the Middle East.

Cisco provides its support personnel and sales reps a great deal of latitude and flexibility to make on-the-spot decisions, no matter how unconventional they may be. In some instances, junior employees with intimate customer knowledge will take charge of critical situations, even if it means elbowing more senior ranking executives out of the way.

"What carries a meeting is the person who spoke to the customer last and knows them best, not the one with the fanciest PowerPoint slides or the most impressive title," says Pinto.

As a result of its focus on customers, Cisco's profitability remains among the highest in the industry. And its customer loyalty, as measured again by Walker Research, is significantly higher than that of the average technology company—almost 80 percent versus mid-50 percent, respectively.

For all the benefits that Cisco has derived from its customer-centricity, its ability to scale would not be possible without the help of business partners. Here's the story of how Cisco created momentum for its business partners and how it unlocked additional value for itself by doing so. Given the backdrop of the story, the solution arrived not a moment too soon.

From Volume to Value

Shortly before the dawn of the new millennium, Cisco bought a company it believed had the next new thing that every business would eventually want and that every rival would wish it had. That company was Selsius, which produced phone systems that worked over the Internet for a fraction of the cost of traditional technology that ran over telephone lines. Eager to extend its reach in the telecommunication market, Cisco paid $145 million for the Dallas-based company.

But there was a problem. Two, actually. The first was Selsius' breakthrough technology, which had a tendency to break down when pushed too hard. That could be fixed with the right engineering investment. The second issue was Cisco's go-to-market channel, or in the case of voice communications equipment, the lack thereof. Cisco had few ties to business partners that sold voice communications products, so growing market share seemed like a tenuous proposition at best. Addressing this problem taught Cisco volumes about working with partners that recommend, sell, or support products to customers on its behalf. In particular, it showed Cisco how important it is to reward its partners adequately without compromising its own long-term goals.

Some background: At Cisco, close to 80 percent of revenue flows through a community of third-party companies, known as the channel. That amounted to nearly $32 billion in fiscal year 2008. Cisco has more than 55,000 channel partners all over the globe today, giving it what is known as a highly leveraged model. Think about it. Alone, Cisco employs more than 15,000 salespeople, but when you factor in those who work for partners, the figure swells to 282,000 worldwide—almost twenty-fold. To put that number into some sort of perspective, this provides Cisco with enough feet on the street to call on every substantial manufacturing company in China and every commercial business in Germany, just to name a few examples. It's a staggering reach.

"Our goal is to have the right partner for the right opportunity every time," says Keith Goodwin, senior vice president of worldwide channels at Cisco.

Channel partners resell virtually every product in the company's portfolio—everything from the most sophisticated CRS-1 routers to small Internet access devices. Those that don't resell products still contribute to the Cisco partner community by offering managed services, professional services, outsourcing services, consulting services, or even software development expertise. This chapter, however, focuses on reseller partners.

While Cisco boasts an award-winning partner program today, the company spent years building it and acknowledges that the program is still a work-in-progress. The reasons are many-fold. Partners' business models change constantly. Likewise, technology evolves, and customer buying habits shift. For these reasons and more, it is extremely difficult for Cisco and its partners to work in perfect harmony year in and year out. But by adhering to basic tenets and adjusting specific policies to suit market conditions, Cisco has grown its business more through partners than what it could have achieved on its own. It hasn't been easy, of course. Cisco has struggled at times to maintain peace with its partners. That's especially true on those occasions when the company's value proposition for partners has appeared less than attractive. IT business partners react unfavorably when they believe that they do not have a level playing field on which to compete. That led to tremendous ill will and frustration in the late 2001–2002 timeframe when the dot-com bubble burst. It was more, Cisco would soon learn, than a mere sign of the times.

After the dot-com meltdown, Cisco partners were enduring the effects of several setbacks all at once. Cisco's business had grown rapidly in the previous years and attracted a great number of resellers.

When the market slowed, however, these resellers suddenly found themselves competing with more partners than ever on a smaller number of deals. In just a few short years, the average number of partners bidding on enterprise deals skyrocketed.

Former Cisco reseller Michael Fong recalls the problem: "Even small deals typically attracted a few local resellers, a national mail order company and even a global service provider like AT&T."

Customers soon recognized that vendors were in a pinch and frankly took advantage of the situation to drive down their costs. With more resellers competing for the attention of fewer customers, it was only a matter of time before a vicious price war erupted. When it did, margins fell through the floor, and partners struggled to make a dime. For some, it was the end of the road. Up to 20 percent of Cisco's resellers dropped out of the business, according to company estimates. Those that remained were fighting with one another and with unauthorized brokers who took to eBay to unload Cisco gear left over from failed dot-com companies.

By then, business was beginning to concentrate among a few larger partners. Of Cisco's 55,000 partners, only 3,000 have achieved high certifications. But the top 10 accounted for over 30 percent of Cisco's total business. This posed a long-term challenge to Cisco's overall channel objective, which was to create a healthy climate for all partners, no matter their size or scope. Doing so, Cisco believed, would enable it to serve the maximum number of customers possible, no matter their size or industry.

Cisco's channel executives huddled with their partners to better understand the problem. The crux of their complaint: Few could make enough money reselling Cisco gear. Cisco recognized that it had to change the economics of its reseller channel if it were to pull out of this downward spiral. After much study, the company concluded that it would have to discard one of the staples of its partner program: volume discounts.

Rewarding those who buy in great quantities with greater discounts is as old a practice as retailing and distribution itself. It's practical, efficient, and intuitive. But was it an effective business policy or an old habit that had outlived its usefulness? Cisco had its doubts, especially after reviewing how larger resellers used their discounts to undermine other, smaller resellers. In several instances, some of Cisco's largest business partners used their volume discounts to buy as much Cisco equipment as possible. Whether working directly or through the channel, Cisco has always maintained its customer focus. The concern in the early 2000s was that large discount partners were moving large volumes quickly, without focusing on the sophisticated pre- and post-sales needs of the customer. At times, Cisco had to step in to ensure the end customer got the value that it needed.

That's what led Cisco to rethink its volume-based discounts in March 2001. Abandoning the structure was hugely controversial because it meant asking some of Cisco's biggest allies to accept different contractual terms unless they were willing to change their ways. But it also turned out to be a fundamental game-changer for the company, especially after several additional program tweaks were added later.

"The truth is that our volume-based rewards program was failing us, particularly since we were interested in having channel partners add value," says Surinder Brar, Cisco's director of channel strategy and programs.

Brar's revelation got the company rethinking about what constituted a "best partner" and what distinguished these companies from others. Were those who destabilized product margins for all really good partners? What about those who toiled in far-flung markets or who served lower-profile customer segments but who nonetheless delivered top-notch service: Were they really less valuable partners? Brar didn't think so.

"It dawned on us that volume isn't the right yardstick by which to rate partners; *value* is," he says. To him, this value could be many things, including the ability to tackle customers' most difficult technical challenges, unrivaled knowledge of a vertical market segment, access to critically important customers, or even the number of specially trained and certified employees a company hires. Companies who could consistently deliver on any of these or other fronts—all of which enable the end customers' success—should be rewarded for the value they brought to bear, he believed, so Cisco radically restructured its tiered volume discount structure.

Cisco, of course, would never have identified this value unless it first recognized the limits of a volume-based distribution model that consolidated benefits among a few very large players. Nor would Cisco have unlocked the value trapped inside the shops of its smaller business partners who added enormous value but were stymied by these few, large players.

"When you create a level playing field at the transaction level, you create an environment where partners compete for business based on their value add," says Brar. When companies do that, he adds, vendors and partners both redirect their focus from extracting gain from one another to providing benefits to customers. "When building a channel program, other vendors typically start from their company outwards, rather than the customer inwards. When we switched the focal point, it triggered a completely different channel strategy."

While revolutionary in theory, Cisco still needed to figure out how to reward those companies that fit this new definition of "best partners." The answer wasn't product discounts but performance rewards. That led to the introduction of incentive programs that compensated partners based on their behaviors. For example, Cisco created programs to reward those who devised complete, end-to-end solutions for customers and those who helped Cisco gain entry into targeted accounts or established a foothold into a new vertical market.

One program, which rewarded partners for their ability to sell new and advanced technology, helped change the trajectory of the entire company. Here's how.

New Math for New Markets

Most newly introduced Cisco products have a built-in following among existing Cisco resellers. But not always. On occasion, Cisco finds itself with a new set of capabilities and no one to sell them. That happened with the aforementioned Selsius acquisition. At the time, there were more than one billion traditional telephones installed around the world. Almost none had a Cisco brand on them. Cisco, of course, wanted to change that.

At the time of the Selsius acquisition, making telephone calls over the Internet was a novel idea, the kind of thing that geeks drooled over but that serious businesses shrugged at. Skype, for example, wouldn't unveil its first Internet phone until August 2003. Cisco, however, was convinced that Voice over Internet Protocol, known as VoIP, would indeed be a huge business. Why? Because the cost of a VoIP system was a fraction of the cost of its traditional PBX counterpart, yet it offered functionality that was better than what traditional voice equipment makers could provide.

VoIP was important to Cisco because it offered the company an opportunity to show existing customers how they could extend the value of their data networks and to show new customers why putting a Cisco network at the center of their technology strategy would pay off handsomely.

Given that the traditional voice market was fragmented both by geography and by manufacturer, Cisco thought the door was open for a breakthrough company offering a disruptive technology. Before it could open that door, however, Cisco needed a more stable product and a cadre of channel partners.

Initially, Cisco discovered that customers were reluctant to commit. No one wanted to risk the rock-solid reliability they enjoyed with traditional phone equipment with unproven technology from a data communications company. The situation seemed right out of Clayton Christensen's *Innovator's Dilemma*, with Cisco, the challenger, trying to enter the market at the low end and then working its way up to take on entrenched leaders.

Undaunted, Cisco did its best to convince customers to try its products. Within a year of delivering a stable product with business-critical features, Cisco VoIP sales began to grow. They totaled approximately $100 million per quarter by late 2002. But then they plateaued. After engaging early adopters and tech-savvy enthusiasts, Cisco found no mass market of follow-up buyers waiting in the wings. The company had single-digit market share and was stuck in the number six position among leading vendors.

Cisco needed a new strategy. In the fall of 2003, Cisco Senior Vice President Don Proctor, general manager of the voice business, brought his quandary to the attention of Cisco's Enterprise Business Council (EBC), a cross-functional executive team responsible for the enterprise business at Cisco. Proctor recognized that the failure of VoIP to gain momentum was a company-wide problem that would require a cross-functional solution. So in October 2003, the EBC convened for an entire day to focus on the VoIP opportunity, which was soon renamed Unified Communications (UC). The debates over strategies, technical requirements, and functional responsibilities waged from the early hours until late in the evening.

One of the key items addressed that day was the complete lack of channel support. A boundary existed between Cisco and its channel partners, and the culprit, said Cisco Senior Vice President Edison Peres, was profitability. Peres, who had a background in the voice industry, stood before the group and painstakingly explained that Cisco's traditional reseller programs provided margins of 8–12 percent to data products resellers. Given the additional money they could charge for valued-added services in the information technology market, these margins on Cisco products were acceptable. But those same numbers didn't work for resellers who worked in the traditional voice world. For business partners in that market, margins typically ran in the 20–25 percent range. Worse for Cisco, its new technology virtually eliminated a lucrative revenue stream for traditional voice resellers: moves, adds, and changes (MAC) to phone systems.

"Unless we change the math, there is no reason for voice resellers to give up their traditional business to help us," Peres told his colleagues. "Nor can we count on existing partners to jump in. They just aren't familiar with voice customers and voice technologies."

As a result, Cisco was effectively blocked from gaining traction in the market, so the council needed to move—and fast. First, it voted to increase spending to recruit voice consultants and analysts who could help influence voice customers on Cisco's behalf. And then the council decided to do the unthinkable: 20 percent of the revenue from every voice product sale would go back to the partner that helped Cisco secure that business.

It was a tough choice: reduce Cisco's own return on investment or allow its partners to suffer and miss a major market transition. After some discussion, Cisco recognized that its long-term need for partners far outweighed any short-term gain. So Cisco met with its partners and shared with them a new idea, the Value Incentive Program (VIP), which was designed to overcome several of these shortcomings. Among other things, VIP paid resellers a fee for every VoIP deal they successfully closed. In most cases, partners could literally double, if not triple, their profitability on any VoIP deal. Overnight, Cisco changed the dynamics of the voice market.

But not everyone was happy. Some inside the company thought it was far too risky to give up so much revenue; others thought the benefit should go to customers, not partners. But the decision stood. For the first time in Cisco history, the company would directly share the proceeds of its sales with partners. That meant asking internal business managers to accept a lower contribution margin in exchange for jump-starting sales. It was not an easy decision, but the company saw it as an opportunity. It changed the economics of partnering by looking at profits end-to-end, across the entire value chain.

Then the council made other changes. To improve customer satisfaction and ensure deployment success, the EBC suggested that every complex deal initially be sold with a services contract. In addition, all product testing would be put through an even more stringent review process than other Cisco products—a systems assurance process to guarantee everything was rock-solid.

These decisions and more—increasing recruitment, boosting marketing, bolstering reseller margins, promoting a service contract sale, and extending product testing—added cost and time to Cisco's sales cycle. But the company felt these measures were absolutely necessary if it were to succeed in selling disruptive voice technology to customers who were accustomed to flawlessly reliable phone service under all but the rarest of circumstances. The council members believed that this would result in both satisfied customers and gratified partners. All of these decisions were mapped to the newly-developed 10-Point Plan, which the council agreed to review and monitor on a regular basis.

Why was this effort so unique? For starters, each council member was empowered to make decisions "at the table." From this stemmed alignment between the vision and the strategy. The council also played a key role with execution: Once each quarter, the council's plan was reviewed by the company's senior-most leaders, including CEO Chambers. Individual names were linked to specific tasks, and those who succeeded were singled out for praise; those who struggled were privately questioned. In addition, the company adopted Cisco IP phones as its standard telephony solution, enabling employees to understand both the promise and the initial limitations of the technology.

In the two years following that October 2003 council meeting, Cisco UC sales rose 40 percent per year. Customer reference accounts stepped forward, and traditional Cisco reseller partners volunteered to invest in training so they could sell the new technology. Eventually, more than 2,000 partners would sign on to deliver UC solutions around the world. Because Cisco focused on rewarding partner investments to meet customer needs, all 2,000 of these partners had an opportunity to profit.

Momentum increased, and Cisco's market share reflected the gains. The company that once languished as sixth in a crowded market moved to the number one position, with more than 30 percent market share.

Building on Momentum

When Cisco changed the economics of its channel programs, it not only improved its relationships with partners, but also gave them the financial strength they needed to make investments of their own to help their end customers. In the last six years, Cisco has paid out more than $2 billion in rewards to partners.

"What Cisco did was simply create additional touch points that cemented relationships up and down the value chain. For example, we increased our involvement with the company in terms of training, product knowledge and direct interfacing with key personnel. When we did, we passed that same value to our customers," says Fong. "As a result, there's greater opportunity that exists between us and Cisco, and between us and our customers. If some other vendor comes along with a single benefit, no one in the value chain is going to jump because there's simply so much residual value in various relationships we have established."

To any vendor that relies on business partners to help it cater to customers, that stickiness is worth its weight in gold. Here's why: Just as unhappy partners often translate into unhappy end user customers, the reverse is also true. Happy partners translate into satisfied customers. Cisco has seen its customer satisfaction scores jump from 4.06 to 4.61 on a 5-point scale since it unveiled VIP.[7] Today, the satisfaction of customers served by Cisco partners is on par, and often *higher*, than the satisfaction of those served by Cisco directly.

Because Cisco enhanced profitability, leveled the playing field, and provided a way for all partners to benefit from a relationship with Cisco, they have increased their commitment to Cisco and its products.

Take World Wide Technology Inc. (WWT), for example. The St. Louis company is one of Cisco's largest Gold partners. But it wasn't always that way. CEO Jim Kavanaugh says Cisco accounted for roughly 10 percent of WWT's sales just a few years ago. At the time, his company generated about $1 billion in total revenue and struggled to make money with the $100 million of Cisco products that it sold.

"Relations weren't great and the sales environment seemed tense. We wondered if we should be looking at alternative vendors," he says. "We really wanted to grow with Cisco; we just couldn't see how."

Then, VIP was introduced. Almost immediately, WWT's salespeople saw a way to make money and began pushing Cisco products like never before. And with profitability on the rise, Kavanaugh fully supported the effort because he saw in Cisco a willingness to listen and adapt.

"There is a level of maturity in the [Cisco] leadership team around their ability to listen. They listen better today and in the last five years than at any time in the history of the business," says Kavanaugh. "They have figured out ways to get into growth markets and take advantage of opportunities in good times and bad. That's someone I want to partner with."

Thanks to the changes Cisco made, Kavanaugh saw his business flourish. Overall sales more than doubled within five years of the introduction of VIP. WWT's sales of Cisco products and services grew 10 times in that same period, eventually accounting for one-third of

WWT's overall revenue. Put another way, by 2008 WWT did as much in Cisco sales as it did in *total* sales before VIP was introduced.[8]

VIP, of course, was only part of the equation for improving relations with partners and launching Cisco into a new technology category. Replacing its volume-based model with a value-based one helped immensely. "A model that produces lower margins translates into reduced partner satisfaction, which leads to crummy customer satisfaction. Nobody wins when that happens," says Goodwin.

There are several other noteworthy things that Cisco did to help build on this momentum. For example, the company began huddling with key partners and jointly drafting business plans and go-to-market strategies. Cisco also provided financial guidance and expertise to partners so that they could better manage their money and investments. And then, to make sure that it was addressing their concerns on a more frequent, ongoing basis, the company began hosting Cisco Partner Executive Exchange (CPEE) conferences around the world. At these events, the company gathered its best partners from a variety of markets and discussed with them what was working and what was not. The events gave partners an opportunity to voice concerns in an open, collaborative environment and to solicit Cisco's immediate feedback in real time.

The results: Customer satisfaction up from 4.06 to 4.61. Profitable business with World Wide Technology from $100 million to nearly $1 billion. Unified Communications market position up from number six to number one.

Those are numbers even Lexus would be proud of.

6

The Beaten Path *and* The Road Less Traveled

Established and Emerging Countries

A single millimeter.

That's all it took to sink the Whirlpool Corporation's dream of developing a washing machine that would serve the needs of customers from Mumbai to Mexico City.

The time was 1990, when going "global" held the promise of hundreds of millions of new customers for executives of Western companies from developed lands. The lure of the emerging world and all its upside was irresistible for many, including then Whirlpool CEO David Whitwam. "Being an international company—selling globally, having global brands or operations in different countries—isn't enough," he told the Harvard Business Review in 1994, "Everybody is going global but hardly anyone understands what it means."[1]

To Whirlpool, it meant the "World Washer"—a slimmed down, simplified washing machine that could be sold globally with minimal localization.[2] The device reflected the company's strategy of using a common product design all over the world, in order to create never-before-realized economies of scale. Whitwam believed that this could help save the Benton Harbor, Michigan, company $200 million annually within a few short years.[3]

Despite all its efforts to perfect this relatively simple design, Whirlpool missed the mark by less than the width of a paper clip. But it may as well have been 5,000 kilometers.

A single millimeter gap between the agitator and the drum of the machine was the culprit. This gap was perfectly fine in the United States, where people laundered durable clothing like jeans and t-shirts, but it was ill-suited for India, where the machines had to accommodate saris. The long, thin fabric would get stuck in the one-millimeter gap, destroying the delicate garments.

The setback cost Whirlpool not only goodwill in the Indian market, but lost opportunities as well. Buffeted by complaints by numerous consumers, the company had to rethink its product strategy and then pay a Korean company for its designs for a replacement product launch.[4]

To this very day, the World Washer is held up as one of many examples of failed attempts by Western companies to transport products and strategies crafted in established markets to emerging markets. In the case of the World Washer, it turned out to be too expensive for India, and at least as far as saris were concerned, too aggressive.

What does the story of Whirlpool tell us?

That strategies and products developed for the United States and Western Europe don't always work in places such as India, where needs, expectations, and means are very different. That goes for China, Africa, and Latin America as well.

The inverse is also true.

Phone giant Nokia is excelling in the emerging markets, thanks to its pioneering endeavors. By lining up key distribution agreements and introducing innovative solutions, such as cell phones with integrated radios and flashlights, the company has addressed the needs of local customers in India.[5] As a result, it has established a commanding 55 percent share of the market,[6] which boasts more than 525 million mobile subscribers.[7] And to better understand the needs of its customers in emerging countries, Nokia operates "Open Studios" in places such as Brazil, Ghana, and India, where it invites local developers to share their ideas for new designs and features. In April 2008, *BusinessWeek* magazine showcased some designs, which included solar charging cells and ozone monitors for measuring pollution in crowded urban areas.[8]

While Nokia was focused on emerging markets, it took its eye off the ball in the established world, where a smartphone revolution was underway. In addition to basic phone features, customers there also wanted applications, web browsing, and global positioning systems available on devices like Apple's iPhone and RIM's Blackberry. Nokia's inability to meet customer needs in both established and emerging countries resulted in a significant drop in its smartphone market share, from almost 51 percent in the fourth quarter of 2007 to less than 41 percent in the fourth quarter of 2008.[9]

Where Whirlpool succeeded in established countries, and Nokia succeeded in emerging markets, some companies are learning to do both.

Take General Electric, for example. It was challenged when it first tried to sell sophisticated medical equipment in China in the late 1990s. Rather than give up on the market, however, GE decided to make an even bigger commitment to China with new technologies designed specifically for that market. One piece of diagnostic scanning equipment that GE designed for the Chinese market, for example, costs one-third of what its original counterpart costs in the United States and Europe. When it achieved the leading market share in China, GE introduced the product in more established countries and marketed it to thousands of health care facilities that could not afford its original, core offering. By serving the Chinese market with a customized product and applying what it learned in the United States, GE did both—established countries and emerging countries.[10]

The crux of GE's success is that its strategy and business model for the emerging countries were distinct from, yet complementary to, its strategy and business model in the established world. Better yet, the two leveraged one another to produce new gains.

GE CEO Jeffrey Immelt described his company's approach in an October 2009 article for the *Harvard Business Review*. "The reality is, developing countries aren't following the same path and could actually jump ahead of developed countries because of their greater willingness to adopt breakthrough innovations. With far smaller per capita incomes, developing countries are more than happy with high-tech solutions that deliver decent performance at an ultralow cost—a 50 percent solution at a 15 percent price. And they lack many of the legacy infrastructures of the developed world, which were built when conditions were very different. They need communications, energy, and transportation products that address today's challenges and opportunities, such as unpredictable oil prices and ubiquitous wireless technologies."[11]

Like GE, Cisco did business in emerging countries for years—and did fairly well there. But it didn't see a significant increase in influence or relevancy until the company's leaders stepped back and examined the real opportunity in the emerging world. Cisco was forced to examine everything from product offerings to pricing models to go-to-market strategies to hiring policies and more. What the company concluded was that emerging countries moved with different rhythms and often with different objectives than their counterparts in more established countries. Unless Cisco made a commitment to understand these conditions, its leaders conceded, it would never fully maximize its opportunities there.

Cisco already had sales offices, manufacturing facilities, and distribution hubs in many emerging countries. These gave the company *presence*, but CEO John Chambers wanted greater *relevance* with national, business, and academic leaders. Instead of settling for a role as an IT supplier to emerging countries, he believed that Cisco could become a key, trusted advisor.

So the company began formulating an approach to emerging countries that was unlike anything it had done before. Considering the changes underway in the world's economy, the timing couldn't have been better.

Boldly Going Where Few Had Succeeded Before

At the dawn of the new millennium, it became clear that the combined economic output of the world's emerging economies would soon surpass that of the world's established nations. Experts now predict this will occur in the next few years.[12] Cisco recognized this global economic shift would mean several things. For starters, there would be hundreds of billions of dollars up for grabs.[13] Some of that would come from investments that individual nations were planning to make on infrastructure upgrades that they believed could help their economies catch up to, if not leapfrog, those of the West. Some would come from the development funds that institutions such as the European Union (EU), World Bank, and International Monetary Fund (IMF) were making available to emerging economies. And finally, even more would come from the billion new consumers expected to enter the market for the first time.

A Goldman Sachs study calculates that the global middle class—which it defines as people with annual incomes ranging from $6,000–$30,000—is growing by 70 million people a year.[14] These consumers need everything from communications to transportation to housing to take their place in the world economy.

To prepare for this, Cisco needed to rethink its approach to emerging countries. That meant devising entirely new strategies for the nations that boast more than 85 percent of the world's oil reserves,[15,16] more than 85 percent of its natural gas,[17] and more than 75 percent of its copper,[18] along with a growing number of world-class business and educational institutions. If Cisco were to distinguish itself from the many others who noticed the upsurge in economic activity in these nations—including an estimated $21.7 trillion in infrastructure spending by 2018—it would have to demonstrate a relevance that matched its interest.[19]

Cisco understood that emerging countries—from behemoths like China and India, to smaller markets such as Poland, Argentina, and Egypt—have different needs than mature markets. But catering to those was difficult for Cisco, given its organizational structure at the time. For example, the territory manager responsible for sales in Italy was also responsible for sales in neighboring Croatia and Bosnia-Herzegovina. As you can imagine, the manager devoted more of his time to the world's tenth largest economy than he did to the world's 68th and 97th largest economies.

The first step in overcoming this natural tendency? Separate emerging countries from traditional sales territories and elevate their priority inside the company.

In August 2005, Executive Vice President Rick Justice established a new region for the emerging markets. With this, Cisco sent a signal to the outside world that it was serious about emerging countries and told employees that they could no longer fall on old familiar ways of doing business. The new geography was composed of countries culled from Latin America, Russia, the Commonwealth of Independent States, the Middle East, Africa, and Central and Eastern Europe.

To minimize disruption in Asia, Cisco maintained the composition of its Asia Pacific region, which included India, China, and several other emerging and developed countries. To lead its charge into these countries, Senior Vice President Owen Chan continued to lead the Asia Pacific region, and Senior Vice President Paul Mountford was appointed to lead the emerging markets region.

The product of a hardscrabble, factory town in England, Mountford seemed like an ideal choice to lead Cisco into places where it had never gone before. Gregarious and competitive, he made a decision as a young man not to tether his future to his town's 200-year-old ironworks and steel factory. Instead, he joined the computer revolution.

Upon taking over as head of Cisco's newly christened emerging markets region, Mountford started to devise a unique strategy.

He understood that Cisco needed a balance of insiders and external partners to adequately cover the region. So he began hiring country managers who were, for the most part, natives of the countries they served. His team also began recruiting new partners and solidifying relationships with existing ones. Mountford began amassing reams of economic, political, and social data on more than 130 countries. This helped his team shape its coverage model plans and draft their go-to-market strategies.

The emerging markets team started to build locally relevant solutions tailored specifically for customers in emerging markets. That included special offerings tailor-made to help municipalities create "Digital Cities" and connect health care providers, among other things. Given the construction booms underway in the Middle East, Africa, and Russia, Mountford's team also began compiling solutions for specific vertical markets, with a particular focus on tourism, real estate, construction, and transportation industries. Some ideas came from customers themselves. Could Cisco replicate the airport solution that it devised for the city of Toronto to help the city of Dubai? That's what the former CIO from Toronto wanted to know when he called Cisco after accepting the same job in the United Arab Emirates.

Cisco could achieve a sizeable return by establishing a presence in the emerging market countries, and the company could boost this return with locally relevant solutions. But Mountford knew that the lynchpin for Cisco's success would be whether or not the company could participate in the broad country transformations underway in many emerging nations. He recognized that unless Cisco played a significant role in the ongoing infrastructure, financial and social transformations in the emerging countries, the company would be seen as just another Western company looking to make a quick buck in a new land. So he began calling on heads of state, along with ministers of communication, transportation, healthcare, and education. He huddled with business leaders, academics, and other influential figures to learn about their challenges and goals. His message: Technology investments lead to productivity gains, which translates into economic growth and therefore in a rise in living standards.

"Selling products was obviously very important to Cisco," says Mountford. "But we recognized early on that we had a unique opportunity to participate in country transformation at a very high level. That meant helping emerging countries develop blueprints for increasing social and digital inclusion, and tackling some of the bigger issues before them."

Hitting Bumps in the Increasingly Flat, Digital World

With its three-pronged plan—presence, relevance, and country transformation—in place, Cisco expected to build momentum rapidly in places such as Romania, Mexico, and the United Arab Emirates, but it quickly encountered roadblocks, both externally and internally.

The sheer challenges associated with setting up a local infrastructure proved more difficult than originally anticipated. Some of that was due to the difficulties in dealing with government regulators or local business officials. But much of it had to deal with Cisco itself. Just to establish a new office in an emerging country required the coordination of 22 separate business functions inside Cisco. There were legal issues to solve, offices to rent, staffing challenges to address, IT systems to install, and licenses to obtain, among other things. For a newcomer to Cisco (and most county managers were newcomers since Cisco was expanding), the burden was almost overwhelming. Mountford soon discovered that his new country managers were spending 80 percent of their time setting up local infrastructure and just 20 percent with customers.

Meanwhile, Chan faced similar challenges with the emerging economies in the Asia-Pacific region: Opening offices in Western China, localizing products for emerging countries, and recruiting the best talent all proved to be obstacles that he had to overcome.

Mountford and Chan, along with Senior Vice President (and author) Inder Sidhu, believed that Cisco could overcome its challenges with the emerging markets if the country managers in far-flung locales had better support from and access to corporate resources.

The three executives recognized Cisco's processes were geared for the company's biggest opportunities and most mature operations. But the ability to work on relatively small issues in far-off lands? This was a challenge. And the further out in emerging countries that Cisco reached, the more issues there seemed to be. What is the best way to serve customers who speak Pashto, trade in Afghanis, and have technology needs in Afghanistan, where you need clearance from the U.S. Department of Defense just to make contact? That's a real issue Cisco faced. And it was just one of dozens like that.

To address these issues, the Emerging Countries Council (ECC) was born in early 2006, with Sidhu, Mountford, and Chan as co-leaders.

The ECC—one of nine cross-functional leadership teams formed around Cisco's $10 billion market opportunities—quickly set the audacious goal of tripling the business in just five years, or reaching a run rate of $10 billion in annual revenue in a matter of a few short years. But first, the ECC had to help emerging countries scale operations and install the support mechanisms required to do business around the world.

Sidhu, Mountford, and Chan drafted some of the company's top executives from operations and finance, government relations, corporate philanthropy, and acquisitions to serve on the new council. The ECC leaders recruited three of Cisco's six executive vice presidents and some of its most influential leaders from the worlds of sales, services, operations, planning, manufacturing, human resources, and marketing. This included Senior Vice President of Corporate Affairs Tae Yoo, Senior Vice President of Manufacturing Angel Mendez, and Chief Financial Officer Frank Calderoni.

Membership and vision established, the council got down to business. Council members began to spend significant time in places like India, Russia, China, and the Middle East. They removed obstacles, garnered funding and resources, and helped establish infrastructure. Most importantly, the ECC educated leaders within the company as to the real opportunity in the emerging countries and the actions required to capture it.

Progress was swift. In its first full year, the emerging countries business grew by more than 30 percent. Almost as soon as Cisco could install salespeople into a new region and equip them, bookings followed. The number of sales offices grew as well, from 45 countries in 2005 to 59 by 2006.

By the time the ECC moved into its second year of operations, it began shifting from reactive to proactive initiatives. Supply lines were established, accountability was institutionalized, and functions were aligned. But the company still needed answers for dealing with the spiraling need for corporate resources, including services, IT, human resources, and legal.

The ECC jumped in to help. Instead of simply requesting more budget or headcount, the council actually identified the investments required to grow revenue by a designated amount. This approach got results: In a year of tight budgets, the council secured an additional $58 million for the emerging countries in 2007. The ECC then applied these funds to fortifying the central functions, in support of the field. This represented the first end-to-end value chain for the emerging countries, which soon added another 17 nations to its portfolio.

Moving into its next phase, the ECC decided to rally the company around its efforts in specific countries, starting with Mexico.

The council decided to address a longstanding shortcoming in Cisco strategy in Mexico—the company was only doing business with a few of the 18 families who, along with the government, influence 65 percent of the country's GDP. The council began a concerted effort to forge relationships with these families, including a trip to Mexico in 2008. One of the people the council met with during this visit was Alejandro Burillo Azcárraga, chairman of Grupo Pegaso. He was so enamored by the description of Cisco TelePresence technology that he asked for systems at his home in Vail, Colorado, his office in Mexico City, and even on his yacht. (No word yet when the marine-ready version of Cisco TelePresence will be available, but a consumer version was announced in January 2010.)

After creating ties to key influencers in Mexico, Cisco then focused its energies on developing strategies to help the country address some of its most pressing challenges in the areas of health and safety, education, and citizen inclusion. These efforts culminated in the signing of Memoranda of Understanding with three state ministries in April 2009. The signing of the accord took place at an event attended by Mexico President Felipe Calderon and Cisco CEO John Chambers. There, Chambers unveiled Cisco's largest commitment to the nation to date: a plan to invest as much as $5 billion in technology, training, and infrastructure. Additionally, Calderon and Chambers committed to making the Mexican government the most connected in the world by 2010. They are already on their way to making that commitment a reality: Cisco has already deployed more than 30 TelePresence rooms across 2 dozen different ministries and agencies in the Mexican government.

In addition to the investments Cisco is making in Mexico, the ECC is pursuing a similar model in China, including a $16 billion investment, and is expanding the idea to India, Russia, Brazil, and beyond.

As Cisco grows its business in these emerging countries, it also endeavors to transfer knowledge from the emerging world back to the established. Here's how.

Leveraging the Best the World Has to Offer

Two weeks before the motion picture *Slumdog Millionaire* stunned the world by winning the Oscar for Best Picture, a new initiative was launched in India to address some of the challenges that result from rapid urbanization, as seen in the film. That effort is Cisco Smart Connected Communities.

Working with partners around the globe, Cisco is developing technologies that will help municipal leaders to better manage their communities. How? By connecting citizens, resources, and institutions in urban settings, which are literally teeming with people. Take Mumbai, for example, the setting of the award-winning film.

The population of Mumbai has grown seven-fold since 1950. And its growth continues unabated. By 2015, the city is expected to add another two million residents.[20] That's like adding another city the size of Las Vegas or Vancouver.[21] But the growth doesn't end with India. Thirty of the world's fastest growing cities are located in emerging countries, in places such as Rwanda, Mexico, Venezuela, Niger, and the Congo.[22] United Nations estimates suggest that 500 million people will become urbanized within the next five years.

All this growth is adding up to a lot of challenges for community and world leaders, who are well-aware that the current infrastructure in these cities is woefully unprepared to handle such a surge. "More than ever before, cities are home to humanity's great expectations," said a United Nations Habitat Report in 2008. "They are also home to increasing social disparities, poverty, pollution, waste and environmental problems."[23]

To combat these challenges, leaders are investing hundreds of billions of dollars in infrastructure—everything from roads to sewers to airports and more. In addition to all the brick and mortar they are buying, they are dramatically stepping up their investments in information and communications technologies.

That's why Cisco created Smart Connected Communities, an integrated set of network-based solutions that improve economic development, city management, and quality of life for citizens around the world. "Smart Connected Communities puts the network at the center of city planning and management," says Executive Vice President Wim Elfrink. "By running a city on networked information, leaders and citizens alike can connect and share information in real time."

By embedding networking technology in buildings, public safety systems, transportation systems, and a myriad other things, Cisco can help community leaders offer remote healthcare services, increasing the availability of preventative care. They can automate and remotely monitor building security, thus improving safety and lowering costs. They can provide real-time traffic information and therefore reduce greenhouse gas emissions.

But that's not all. Smart Connected Communities is also making a difference in rural settings in underdeveloped areas, providing villagers and nomadic people with technology such as the mobile Internet. With these solutions, services like personal finance, healthcare, education, and more will be available to people in some of the furthest reaches in the world.

Among the notable things about the Smart Connected Communities solution is where it is developed. Instead of San Jose, Raleigh, London, or some other engineering lab in the developed world, it is being developed where it is needed most—in the heart of the emerging world, where it is most relevant today.

The level of innovation emanating from the emerging countries convinced Cisco to invest more there, not just to sell gear, but to capture ideas created there and turn them into solutions—like Smart Connected Communities—that would be relevant all over the world.

To make the most of this opportunity, Cisco built a second world headquarters in Bangalore, India in 2007. The man who oversees this effort at Cisco is Elfrink. A native Dutchman, Elfrink speaks eight different languages and has lived most of his adult life in places other than the Netherlands. And as the head of Cisco's $8 billion services business, he has experience running large, complex operations and dealing with the media to boot. To underscore the importance of his new assignment, Cisco named Elfrink Chief Globalization Officer before sending him to the subcontinent.

At the time, Cisco was not aware of any other company that had such a position. But Chambers thought the title would underscore just how serious Cisco was about developing global capabilities. From the onset, he tasked Elfrink with building Cisco's operations in Bangalore as a center of excellence that could launch customer solutions development and services delivery for the emerging world and beyond.

"We want to build the company for speed, scale, flexibility and replicability," says Elfrink. "This is what globalization provides to the company."

Elfrink believes that at least 20 percent of Cisco's leadership talent will be based outside of the United States, Europe, and other established economies. He says it is incumbent for forward-thinking companies to look to places such as India for growth, innovation, and talent.

Inaugurated in November 2007, the Cisco Globalization Center is today an epicenter of solutions development, product development and localization, and technical support, as well as a growing destination center for leading entrepreneurs, consultants, and networking engineers. More than just another office, it is a second company headquarters that plays a critical role in the company's transformation from a multinational corporation to a global innovator. The home of key business functions inside the company, the Globalization Center has 5,000 workers and expects that number to double over the next several years.

Close geographically and culturally to many of the emerging countries, India has become a key hub of solutions development for—and engagement with—many of these countries. This is providing Cisco a level of relevance that the company has never before enjoyed in many parts of the world.

"Don't sell what you have," says Elfrink of his philosophy for customizing solutions for customers in the emerging countries. "Create what they need."

That's a big change for Cisco's salespeople, who credit the Globalization Center for helping them win back business once lost to the rivals who demonstrated greater local industry know-how than Cisco.

"Before the Globalization Center, we were limited in terms of what we could provide to customers," says Ferry Chung, director of business development for Cisco's Asia Pacific region. "But when the Globalization Center opened and we saw the programming and integration work they could do, we formed an Internet Solutions Group here in Asia to leverage work done in India. We now have the support we need to provide real solutions to customers in fields such as real estate, healthcare and manufacturing."

The result? More functionality for customers and more business for Cisco. Take SingHealth, the largest healthcare group in Singapore, for example. Cisco created a Connected Healthcare solution that dramatically increased the number of patients that the healthcare provider could reach remotely using Internet technology. SingHealth rewarded Cisco for the effort by increasing its spending on Cisco products and services by a factor of five.

This kind of success has inspired Cisco to make other bets in emerging countries that wouldn't be possible without Elfrink's team. Take the Connected Real Estate solution, for example. It is helping building owners better manage their facilities by linking disparate power, lighting, plumbing, heating, and cooling systems over a single network. The core solution was developed in the Globalization Center and then shared with Cisco teams in Asia and the Middle East, where a great deal of the world's new construction is ongoing.

Keen customer interest in Connected Real Estate inspired Cisco to make an even larger commitment to this market in January 2009, when it acquired Richards-Zeta Building Intelligence. In past years, Cisco would never have dreamt of pursuing a company that developed such specific industry solutions. But now that it has the Globalization Center, it can. Today, important business units at Cisco are taking shape in India. For example, the Converged Building Systems Business Unit, of which Richards-Zeta is now part, is based in Bangalore—a business unit based in an emerging country with the specific charter of building products for the rest of the world.

This kind of effort is helping to make Cisco an influential player in industries where the company was traditionally an afterthought. None of this would be possible without Cisco's devotion to making the most of opportunities in emerging countries.

"It's fair to say that no one has gone to the extent that Cisco has to develop transformative industry solutions in the emerging world with an eye to migrate them back to the established world," says Savi Baveja, a consultant with Bain & Company.

Baveja has studied the globalization efforts of companies like IBM, Motorola, and Nokia. Several have progressed well beyond basic labor arbitrage and market expansion and are now considered innovators in their fields. While many companies pursue productivity, scale, market opportunities, business model innovation, skills development, and/or risk management in emerging countries, very few progress beyond a basic level in any one of these areas. Even world-class leaders who have been at it for more than a decade—Accenture, for example—have developed advanced capabilities in only a few of these areas. But Cisco, in a relatively short time, has made remarkable progress, Baveja believes.

Because it didn't form its globalization strategy until the middle of this decade, Cisco is doing what many organizations and institutions in emerging countries are themselves attempting, that is, a leapfrog jump over those with a more established presence in emerging countries. To do that, Cisco recognizes that it will need to do something that sets it apart from its predecessors, many of whom stopped investing in emerging countries once they established sales offices or offshore labor centers. Cisco believes continued investment with an eye on cross-leveraging efforts between emerging and established countries will provide it the edge that it seeks.

"Whether it is Dubai, Shanghai, or Mumbai, Cisco is more relevant in the emerging world thanks to the Globalization Center," says Elfrink. "Every day, that relevance spreads back to the established world and beyond. For instance, our Smart Connected Communities solution is now being adopted in San Francisco and Toronto."

While Cisco's efforts may not be worthy of something akin to an Oscar just yet, the company is pleased that it has proven to customers and thought leaders all over the world that it is something altogether different than a mere market contestant hoping to be the next "millionaire."

Ideas Without Borders

A cheap labor pool. A place to peddle inexpensive merchandise.

That's the way a lot of companies see the emerging world. But Cisco and GE have seen more. And since its debacle with the World Washer, so has Whirlpool.

After its initial setbacks in India, Whirlpool recommitted to the marketplace. In 1996, it bought a 436,000 square foot plant and made an $80 million investment in the facility, which produces refrigerators, washing machines, air conditioners, and microwave ovens. By 2002, Whirlpool had become the top-selling refrigerator and washing machine brand in the country.

But it's not just a capital investment. Whirlpool is learning to do both—emerging *and* established countries. It set up a design center in the Indian state of Maharashtra, which provides services to counterparts in Brazil, Italy, and the United States.

"India is an important market, and by gaining leadership in this market we are today in a position to transfer our learnings to other parts of the world," says Raj Jain, Whirlpool's managing director in India. "As Asian competitors become more visible in other parts of the world, we can understand them and be better prepared for them."[24]

By establishing presence, driving relevance, and striving for country transformation, Cisco expects to do no less.

It isn't abandoning the beaten path, but it also hopes to take the road less traveled.

7

Doing Things Right *and* Doing What Matters
Excellence and Relevance

"A truly 21st century idea." "Bigger than the Internet." "More important than the personal computer."

These were just a few of the early impressions of the Segway Personal Transporter, one of the most celebrated innovations of the last several decades. The first technological marvel of the new millennium, the scooter was expected to revolutionize transportation. Inventor Dean Kamen predicted his two-wheeled device would be to the car "what the car was to the horse and buggy."[1]

So much for great expectations.

When the much anticipated invention went on sale in 2002, the public yawned. Shortly thereafter, new-age observer *Wired* magazine went so far as to sneer, "It would be premature to call the most-talked about scooter in the history of human-kind a huge bust. But the Segway has always been ahead of its time."[2]

Ouch.

Nearly a decade after its unveiling, it's clear to most that the Segway has not changed the way cities are designed, nor the way people get around their neighborhoods. Aside from mall and airport security personnel and a relative handful of postal workers, the Segway is a curiosity to most, a nuisance to others. Even environmentally conscious and technologically progressive San Francisco ruled against the

Segway in 2002, when city officials voted to ban the device from the city's sidewalks due to safety concerns.[3]

So where did Segway go wrong? Certainly not in the design or execution of the two-wheeled device, which is a true marvel. Ingeniously conceived, the Segway overcomes numerous technological challenges, not the least of which is staying upright and safe under the most challenging of circumstances. The Segway can calculate a user's center of gravity 100 times per second and operate in all kinds of weather.[4] It can move along at a top speed of 13 miles per hour—roughly what a world-class marathoner achieves—and stop on a dime. The device produces no carbon emissions and requires little training to operate. And yet it's a commercial flop.

Consider: The Segway factory was designed to produce 40,000 units per month. As of August 2009, however, only 50,000 Segway scooters had been sold—a tiny fraction of original expectations.[5] To say the device has underperformed is an understatement, especially when you consider the high profile of some of its backers. Amazon.com founder Jeff Bezos, for one, called the scooter, "one of the most famous and anticipated product introductions of all time." Silicon Valley investor and serial entrepreneur John Doerr, likewise, had similarly high hopes for the device. He famously predicted that Segway would be the fastest company in history to reach $1 billion in sales.

That didn't happen, of course. Why? For all its technical excellence, the Segway scooter failed to prove its relevance to customers.

Despite the tens of millions of dollars that it took to develop and the patented innovations that were required to produce it, the heavy and over-priced Segway turned out to be a niche product at best, ably helping service workers and public safety professionals in a variety of settings, but hardly changing the world.

That may never have happened had the Segway proven relevant to customers. But relevance simply wasn't as attainable as excellence.

Ironically, a similar fate often awaits those who achieve relevance without excellence. Take the companies behind plastic recycling, for example. In these environmentally conscious times, what could be more relevant? Despite overwhelming interest, however, less than 1 percent of all polystyrene containers like yogurt cups are recycled in the United States today.[6]

The reason is simple: There's no excellence in the process.

Polystyrene is difficult to separate from other forms of plastic and thus confounds consumers, even environmentally conscious ones. It also requires extensive cleaning and special equipment to process and produces its own greenhouse emissions. In addition, the economics of polystyrene recycling don't yet add up for many of those trying to make a business of it. One ton of this material sells for less than $1,000 and commands much less on the open, scrap market. Given that widely used foam versions of the product are 98 percent air, a ton requires a vast amount of storage space and trucking resources, further diminishing the value of collecting it.

In the last decade, many companies that have tried to make money from recycling polystyrene have failed, and entire cities have given up collecting it. Even environmentalists in some of the country's most progressive communities have been forced to concede defeat. That includes the NextStep Recycling center in Eugene, Oregon, for example. "We wish we could continue to provide this much needed service for our community, but we are losing money with every piece of foam we accept," says Lorraine Kerwood, executive director at NextStep.[7]

While recycling processes are improving, the sad fact remains, as *Popular Mechanics* magazine summarized in 2008, "Most of the plastic put in recycling bins ends up in the garbage."

What the backers of plastic recycling have come to learn is a lesson that Segway knows all too well: It is impossible for an organization or industry to reach its full potential without *both* excellence *and* relevance.

Focusing on one at the expense of the other is simply bad business.

Cisco, too, had to learn this lesson.

Like the company behind the Segway scooter, Cisco had a harder time achieving broad relevance than it did demonstrating excellence. The latter didn't come effortlessly—quite to the contrary—but it was achieved first.

As the world's most successful manufacturer of computer networking equipment, Cisco provides the bulk of the infrastructure that powers the Internet and other networks, both public and private. When you send an email, visit a web page, connect to a secured corporate network or, increasingly, make a simple phone call, chances are Cisco equipment or software made it happen.

As a reminder, Cisco sells products and services to customers of all sizes and does business in more than 140 countries. In its 25 years of business, the company has made more than 130 acquisitions, been named to the top of countless lists of best places to work for, and risen to the top of the corporate world. The company is number 57 on the *Fortune 500* list of the largest industrial companies[8] and has a market capitalization, as of writing, of more than $140 billion.

With innovations like the Cisco CRS-1 Router, which can download the entire printed collection of the United States Library of Congress in just 4.6 seconds (a feat that would take 82 years with a dial-up modem), Cisco continues to demonstrate this excellence today.[9] Cisco is number one or number two in every market and technology category in which it competes.

But for all its excellence, Cisco wasn't always relevant with business decision-makers. IT executives, of course, regarded it as an important supplier of technology for connecting different electronic devices inside their organizations. But CEOs, CFOs, and other business leaders didn't look for inspiring or transformational ideas in the wiring closet.

This is the story of how Cisco set out to make itself more relevant. How did the company do it? By zeroing in on what matters most to customers. Put another way, Cisco became *excellent* by focusing on customer pain points. But it became *relevant* by moving from customer frustrations to their aspirations. While the journey continues to this day, the story began in a more humble time when the Internet was new, and the possibilities seemed endless.

Walk, Then Run: The First Steps on the Road to Relevancy

Though it seems eons ago, you might still remember the first time you logged onto the Internet. For many people, that was probably in the mid-1990s. Then, there were only a handful of web sites that seemed worth your time. But they were enough to make most of us stop and think: "Wow: This changes everything."

Sure enough, the Internet did. Within a few short years of becoming widely available to most businesses and consumers, the Internet changed the way we researched, communicated, and shopped, among other things. These early years of the Internet were characterized by the introduction of technologies that paved the way for greater transactional efficiency and improved data collection and dissemination. Thanks to the Internet, individuals could connect directly to information—almost all the world had ever amassed and stored—for the first time in recorded history.

Cisco, of course, benefited handsomely from this phenomenon. But while its sales and market capitalization grew to record heights, its relevance lagged. CEOs and other business leaders perceived the technology upstart as a worthwhile vendor, but not necessarily a thought leader that could transform their businesses. Most of their focus was directed at the traditional aspects of their operations, which networking technology had yet to transform.

Cisco believed that it could resonate with business decision-makers if it could show them how an organization that leveraged networking technology could increase its productivity, better serve customers, and improve its competitiveness. Unfortunately for Cisco, there were no good examples of this at the time. Various organizations were doing interesting things with the Internet, but no major company had gambled to run the key functions of its business with networking technology. So Cisco CEO John Chambers told his lieutenants that Cisco would be the first. He pushed them to think creatively and to apply Cisco and other relevant technology to all aspects of the business. That included sales, manufacturing, marketing, finance—everything. If we can't drive our own business results with our technology, he challenged, then how can we expect our customers to do so? In other words, use our technology to drive business results, he said, and our relevance will grow.

Cisco-on-Cisco: Making Technology Relevant

When Cisco first began applying networking technology to its business, it did so in fairly obvious ways. It connected workers to data and to basic services, for example. But then it looked more deeply at its business. Rather than augment manual processes with technology, the company began to transform them with technology.

This led to a new way of doing business at Cisco, otherwise known as Cisco-on-Cisco. It was the company's strategy of using Cisco technology to improve business results. In other words, Cisco ran its own critical business functions using its own technology. The effort led to the creation of a slew of productivity and efficiency applications, especially in the areas of employee self-service, customer support, product configuration, and supply chain management. In time, Cisco came to run its entire business on Internet technology. An internal study pegged the benefits at $960 million annually in the late 1990s.

Take the Cisco web site, for example. Known as Cisco Information Online when it was implemented in the 1990s, it provided online customer support for most inquiries. By 2000, more than 80 percent of all technical support questions were handled directly over the

Web, including many being answered by a community of users, years before the advent of social networking. The company saved $200 million annually by moving support from the phone to the Web. But a more important benefit quickly emerged: The quality and consistency of customer support improved, and customer satisfaction increased at a fraction of the cost.

Cisco also built an extensive online ordering capability where dealers could configure product orders to customers' needs and track them from ordering through manufacturing to delivery. This enhanced the ease of doing business with Cisco and even attracted competing resellers who were fed up with other vendors' phone- and fax-based order-entry systems. As Cisco business quadrupled, the number of customer service representatives stayed relatively flat.

Cisco-on-Cisco, of course, didn't stop with a few e-business applications. In time it grew to include nearly the entire Cisco portfolio. After the company entered the voice market, it replaced all of its traditional desktop phones with those that ran over the Internet instead. Given the relative instability of Internet telephones at the time, the move was quite controversial. But it underscored Cisco's commitment to demonstrating the transformational value that Cisco networking technology could provide. It also allowed the company to fix the stability problems before bringing those phones to market.

The more Internet-enabled solutions Cisco deployed to help run the company, the more customers began asking questions. But instead of mere technical questions, they began seeking answers to business problems. Over time, Cisco-on-Cisco became the most requested presentation in Cisco's customer briefing centers. The gains that Cisco claimed to be getting from "eating its own dog food" began to resonate well beyond customers' IT departments. Cisco was transacting 90 percent of its orders—$60 million per day—over the Internet, and resolving 80 percent of customer support cases through web-based, self-service applications.

Suddenly, business customers saw Cisco in a whole new light.

New Models for a New Era: How Process Drove Relevance

Despite this initial success, Cisco knew that these technological changes would only increase the company's relevance so much. Because of this, Cisco recognized that it would have to drive change deeper inside its organization. That, however, required key *process* changes, including how the company funded IT projects internally. Rather than pay for new initiatives out of a centralized IT pool, Cisco shrunk its IT budget and then reallocated much of that money to individual business units. IT would pay for the things that were central to the entire company and benefited from being done just once, but individual business units and functional teams would be required to allocate funds for individual projects if they wanted IT to complete these projects.

The entire company felt the impact of these client-funded projects, as they came to be known. Among other things, department heads and business leaders changed how they approached the design, development, and deployment of applications and services key to their business functions. With their own dollars on the line, business leaders became more careful about the projects they pursued and more involved in implementing new technology that would drive their business objectives. Like any external Cisco customer, they made sure that any outlay of funds was relevant to their business needs.

Thanks to the introduction of the client-funded model, Cisco drastically reduced the number of wasteful IT projects that received a green light. Furthermore, the projects that did get funding were almost always delivered on time.

As for the budget dollars that the IT department returned to the business? They came pouring back into IT, fully aligned with the business priorities. In fact, IT investment at Cisco actually *increased* when business units began funding their own projects. In less than three years, IT spending as a percent of revenue doubled at the company. And it was being spent on projects relevant to business needs.

Driving a Culture of Accountability

Despite the significant gains Internet technology was bringing to Cisco, including process-related benefits, not every business unit embraced management's desire for the widespread application of Internet technology. Engineering, for example, was reluctant to embrace new Internet-enabled processes for fear they would cause delays in product development.

But Chambers would have none of that. He believed that convincing business leaders of Cisco's relevance would be undermined if he couldn't show them how the technology improved *all* parts of his own company. So he pushed for universal technology adoption throughout Cisco.

To better align leaders with Cisco's goals, he and his leadership team launched a study of the Internet-readiness inside the company. Every senior leader was surveyed on his or her openness and ability to leverage the new technology. Upon completion, Cisco discovered that only one-third of the business units were both willing and able to adopt the new technology. A second third of the company's senior executives believed strongly in the transformative powers of the Internet but lacked the wherewithal to leverage it. The final third of executives, meanwhile, lacked both awareness and basic skills.

For a company once dubbed "most Internet-enabled" by *BusinessWeek*, this was a disappointment. As the world's number one supplier of Internet gear, Cisco's management hoped for higher awareness and interest. But they weren't shocked. Embracing the Internet for personal enjoyment and benefit is one thing; transforming your organization with it is another, they realized. After considering the survey results, Chambers came to believe that *culture* was the real impediment to greater Internet use inside the company. To change that, he introduced the Internet Capabilities Review.

Held twice each year beginning in 2000, the Internet Capabilities Reviews required company leaders to stand before the CEO and their peers and outline how they were leveraging the Internet for business gains. To make the task more meaningful, executives had to benchmark their organizations against those deemed best-in-class by Cisco's own IT department. Chambers expected his team to exceed these benchmarks.

While certain departments struggled with their Internet readiness, the overall progress achieved by these internal sessions was substantial. Virtually every department inside the company eventually developed a cultural affinity with the Internet and all things networkable, while Internet-enabled processes were institutionalized throughout the company.

In time, the Internet Capabilities Reviews were no longer necessary; Cisco was Internet-ready, thanks to the technology, processes, and culture it had put in place.

As a result of these changes, Cisco did indeed elevate its relevance among customers during the first wave of Internet adoption. The first effort made its technology more relevant to the business. The second—client-funded projects—set up a process to ensure the business relevancy of all technology expenditures. And the third, Internet Capabilities Reviews, changed the company's culture to be more agreeable to technology-driven business results.

The combination of the three—*technology, process, and culture*—drove Cisco to a far greater degree of relevance, for itself and for its customers.

Suddenly, the CEOs of the world's largest corporations wanted to learn how the company from the wiring closet transformed its business by embracing Internet technology—and whether Cisco could do the same for them. When Chief Marketing Officer Sue Bostrom led Cisco's business consulting team, she personally met one-on-one with 270 CEOs—many from *Fortune 500* companies—during a single six-month period. And under the leadership of Senior Vice President Gary Bridge, that team—the Cisco Internet Business Solutions Group (IBSG)—continues to drive Cisco's relevance to this day by engaging with senior executives around the world and showing them how to achieve business results through technology.

By the turn of the century, when the company's valuation soared above all others for a brief time, Cisco had achieved the relevance it sought for so long.

But another era of innovation was just beginning. Could the company maintain or perhaps even increase its relevance?

Cisco leaders would soon find out.

Collaboration: The Next Revolution

Collaboration.

You do it when you are instant messaging with a friend, debating politics via Twitter, or exchanging status updates on Facebook. Pretty simple, right?

Maybe not. This single word actually represents a revolution. That revolution builds on the foundation of the Internet, adding functionality that is transforming the nature of work.

At its core, collaboration remains what it has always meant—a process for getting multiple people to work together toward a common goal. But Internet-based technology is now taking collaboration to the next level.

With collaboration technology, an aircraft mechanic can confer with distant engine specialists via video to determine the airworthiness of a particular part. Colleagues in different countries can simultaneously edit the same document despite using disparate technology platforms. And an award-winning Hollywood director can direct a movie without stepping foot on the set.

So what can collaboration do for your business? Plenty.

By empowering your employees through collaboration, you can increase your organization's agility and improve its overall competitiveness. Your employees can use collaboration technology to reduce the time and distance that often separates them from co-workers, customers, and partners. As a result, they can be significantly more productive, no matter where or when they choose to work.

With collaboration technology, businesses can communicate in a more visual and interactive way. They can improve coordination between workers, reduce travel costs, simplify information sharing and improve customer service, among other things.

The timing of these innovations couldn't be better, given how global economics have changed the composition and demographics of today's workforce. Thanks to outsourcing and new market expansion, this workforce is more distributed and more interconnected than ever before. The Economist Intelligence Unit estimates that this year, 62 percent of employees will work with colleagues located in different locations, and by 2011, 30 percent of the global workforce will work outside of a traditional, centralized office.[10]

Cisco recognized that collaboration would be the biggest technology trend of the next decade, driving productivity gains of 5 to 10 percent per year. It created a robust portfolio of collaboration technologies, including TelePresence; WebEx; phones that run over the Internet; devices that produce, distribute, and archive videos; and hardware that can carry, distribute, and manage communications traffic no matter the origin or destination.

Using these technologies internally has helped make Cisco's workforce one of the most distributed, connected, and productive in the world. Employees have experienced—and driven—a cultural revolution of not only information-sharing, but also teamwork and transparency. In the past year alone for example, TelePresence usage has increased 10 times while WebEx conferencing usage has soared by 25 times. Video postings, meanwhile, have grown by more than 11 times on the company's internal site.

More than mere statistics, these gains have translated into real business value for Cisco as the company implemented its own collaboration technology internally—just as it did with the Internet 10 years ago. In 2009, Cisco's IBSG organization calculated the benefits that the company derives annually from its collaboration technology investments.

The total amounted to more than $1 billion per year—striking when you consider that this technology has only been around for a few short years. For a more complete breakdown, see Table 7.1.[11]

TABLE 7.1   Cisco Collaboration Initiatives: Benefits and Costs ($1,168B – $116M = $1,052B net)

Initiative	2009 Benefits ($M)	2009 Costs ($M)
Remote Collaboration	$710.8	$109.5
Telecommuting	$298.7	*
Virtual Experts	$128.6	$4.6
Connected Workplace	$13.0	$1.5
Technical Self-Support	$5.6	$0.1
Internal Video	$11.6	$0.5
Total	**$1,168.30**	**$116.20**

*Included in remote collaboration

If this sounds awfully familiar, you're right. This is exactly what Cisco experienced in the 1990s when the Internet first emerged as a game-changer. You've already seen how Cisco made itself more relevant to customers by adopting its own Internet technology once before.

And now Cisco is doing it again, starting with the way it scales to interact with customers.

Executive Scaling

Sometime in the middle of the decade, Chambers began to realize that traveling the globe to meet heads of state, lunch with important CEOs, and speak at premier events was making it difficult for him to maintain close relationships with the people he needed to connect with most. Chambers figured he needed to remain personally involved with 50 to 100 key customers, including the CEOs of AT&T, General Electric, Procter & Gamble, and Walmart. But his travel schedule and management obligations left him little time for follow-up and even less for brainstorming. Surely, Chambers, concluded, there had to be a better way, and not just for him, but also for his senior leadership team. And, of course, for his customers.

The answer was Cisco TelePresence, a high-definition video collaboration system. With TelePresence, people continents away can meet as though they were sitting around the same conference table—all with the touch of a button.

The arrival of Cisco TelePresence inspired Chambers and his senior leaders to get even closer to Cisco's top customers. Collaboration tools, especially TelePresence, accelerate these relationships. Cisco executives can quickly ramp up their involvement with key accounts and participate in ongoing business reviews with their counterparts.

This transformation has strengthened Cisco like few other efforts in the company's history. Take Chambers, for example. More than saving his back from overnight flights, it has helped him to nurture relationships. Instead of meeting with a CEO one or two times per year, Chambers can huddle virtually with several dozen of them six to ten times per year. Because of the level of rapport that develops with frequent interactions, Chambers can actively engage them in meaningful business discussions. And the same is true not just for his leadership team, but for their counterparts at key customers.

TelePresence, of course, is the closest possible experience to a live meeting. That's because the sound quality is good enough to capture a barely audible sigh. The video, meanwhile, is so clear that you can read the watch of a person sitting across from you who may be, in reality, thousands of miles away.

Since its debut more than two years ago, Cisco has installed more than 700 TelePresence rooms internally. The technology has been used by Cisco employees to conduct more than 700,000 hours of meetings—almost 80 years worth. Because people don't travel for these meetings, TelePresence sessions have saved an estimated 228,000 metric tons of carbon emissions and produced an estimated $423 million in travel cost savings for the company.

In addition to saving time and energy, TelePresence systems have helped increase productivity, too. Cisco estimates that the time saved using TelePresence has produced an estimated $122 million in productivity gains for the company.

That said, not all communications require TelePresence. In many settings, the value of virtualizing an experience isn't so much measured by the audio and video quality of the experience, but rather by the ease and speed at which virtual expertise can be summoned. While TelePresence requires a specifically equipped and available room for all meeting participants, other collaboration tools do not. They can virtualize interactions down to the desktop of every computer in the world. Take the company's WebEx conferencing technology, for example. With WebEx, meeting participants can simultaneously discuss and edit documents, exchange data, or deliver presentations to virtually any computer in the world.

Expert Scaling

Cisco employs thousands of engineers and salespeople to cater to customers and business partners. Product Sales Specialists (PSSs), in particular, play a significant role. They are the people who answer difficult pre-and-post sales questions from customers and partners deploying Cisco products in a dizzying number of permutations and combinations. They respond to questions about technology and architecture, as well as inquires about upgrade offers, order procedures, installation instructions, engineering support, end-of-sales visibility, purchase approval, and delivery information, just to name a few.

And much like Chambers embraced TelePresence, Cisco's PSSs have eagerly adopted WebEx to improve not only their productivity, but their quality of life.

Like most companies, Cisco had a long tradition of sending these experts on the road to meet with partners and customers. For eight years, Cisco's David Farnan was one of those guys. Working approximately 100 miles from the Cisco's headquarters in San Jose, California, Farnan was schooled in a number of Cisco solutions, including Unified Communications. A typical week would see him meet with two or three business partners, often in different cities, and answer questions from others via email. Mostly, he recalls, he spent a lot of his time driving, filling up his gas tank, and grabbing cheap dinners on the road. "I'd travel four, five, maybe even six hours just to meet with a reseller partner for one or two hours. Then I'd head back to the hotel and respond to emails," he says.

When Cisco "virtualized" his expertise, Farnan's productivity went through the roof. He still spends his day attending meetings, sharing his expertise when called upon. Only now he does so from his hometown of Sacramento, California. His tools are his computer, web camera and WebEx. With the help of account managers who transport him virtually into meetings at the very moment he is needed, Farnan answers difficult customer inquires on demand.

The result? A three-fold increase in customer interactions.

But that's not all. Farnan has reduced his travel so much that he can now do things never before imagined. Thanks to WebEx and other collaboration tools, he won back enough time that he was able to coach the Fair Oaks Pumas, his son's soccer team in Folsom, California, to a 6-1-2 record in 2008. For his efforts, Farnan was named league "Coach of the Year."

And he is not alone. Eighty-four percent of salespeople cite positive impact of collaboration technologies. Seventy-eight percent of employees report increased productivity and improved lifestyle.[12]

Today at Cisco, Virtual Experts like Farnan are common through-out the company. Many have found that their horizons have expanded in ways they never dreamt. If the company's best Spanish-speaking software expert in the public sector market is located in Spain, for example, then the Latin America team won't hesitate to include that person in a customer meeting in Argentina. It can all be done at the touch of a button.

Based on the success of these efforts, Cisco expanded its use of collaboration tools in and around the company. One initiative, for example, equipped many of Cisco's top customers with TelePresence. Another created an online communications and information sharing community for partners around the world.

Thanks to these and other efforts, Cisco can better utilize its global workforce in unprecedented ways. Today, for example, it's not uncommon for a business expert working in London on a customer issue in Nairobi to turn to Hyderabad for support and to San Jose for insight.

Customer Scaling

Each year, Cisco hosts a number of events for partners, analysts and, of course, customers. But these are finite in terms of attendance, duration, and impact. They can only accommodate so many people, last for so many days, and resonate for so long.

Cisco believes that collaboration technology can reduce these limitations.

Cisco is changing the way it approaches these big events, including product launches and other company announcements. When the time came to announce its entry into the virtualized data center market in 2009, for example, Cisco created a hybrid event that combined the best of the live and virtual worlds. The result?

Despite the unconventional approach, the Cisco Unified Computing System (UCS) launch had more impact than the 2004 launch of the Cisco Carrier Routing System (CRS), which was brought to market in a more traditional fashion. While there were 100 customers

present for the live CRS announcement, Cisco leveraged collaboration technology to host more than 7,000 customers when it launched
UCS—450 live and 6,600 by TelePresence and WebEx. The launch
ultimately generated 4 billion media hits.[13]

And Cisco did all this for less than 10 percent of the cost of the
CRS launch.

The company is also investing in collaboration technologies that
allow it to engage with a greater number of attendees at its events. In
2009, for example, Cisco increased participation in its annual Partner
Summit by 75 percent when it invited some speakers and attendees
to participate from remote locations via TelePresence. It did so at 50
percent of the cost per attendee and earned higher satisfaction
scores. And instead of a 3-day conference, the virtual event has
become an online community, enabling partners to talk to Cisco and
with each other every day.

But this doesn't stop with big announcements or formal events.
It's something Cisco is doing every day. Take its web site, for example.

"The idea is to create something that would help us 'sell while we
are sleeping,' providing us additional scale in terms of interactions,"
says Sue Bostrom, executive vice president and chief marketing
officer at Cisco.

In support of this vision, Cisco has transformed its web site into a
model of collaboration by increasing its use of video, blogs, click-to-
chat, and other collaboration technologies. As a result, Cisco has seen
its web traffic double since 2007. Today, the site attracts nearly 14
million unique visitors per month.

But users aren't just browsing Cisco's web site. They are actively
engaging with the company and its partners, too. WebEx collaboration tools, for example, not only match potential customers with
Cisco resellers, but allow them to interact and share documents.
Meanwhile, usage of click-to-chat has skyrocketed. Visitors hold an

average of 15 monthly conversations—six times what they did when the technology was introduced two years ago. All of this results in more sales opportunities. Monthly leads generated over the Web doubled from 2008 to 2009.

This success is apparent throughout the industry. Byte Level Research named the Cisco web site one of the top three global web sites in 2010, behind Google and Facebook, but ahead of bellwethers such as Microsoft, Hewlett Packard, and Intel.[14]

Relevant Again

Cisco transformed itself once when it adopted Internet technology in the 1990s. And it is doing so again today with collaboration. While internal success is well and good, Cisco's most important metric is how well it enables these business gains for its customers.

No longer the company behind the wiring closet, Cisco is now a trusted partner to numerous companies who look to it as much for the business relevance it can share as for the technological excellence it can provide. That includes some of the world's most successful companies, including Coca-Cola, General Electric, FedEx, and Procter & Gamble.

More and more, companies like these turn to Cisco for help with expanding into new markets, developing new business models, and, of course, scaling interactions. They do so because they believe that Cisco's technology and expertise can help them become more relevant to their own customers. Take one of the world's oldest and most established financial institutions, for example, HSBC. Though nearly a century and a half old, HSBC is one of the world's most progressive financial institutions. Thanks to technology, the company is able to turn what others would perceive as a liability and use it as an asset. Here's how the company is doing that, with Cisco's help.

Relevance in Action: One Customer's Bold Example

With $146.5 billion in annual sales, HSBC has operations in more than 86 countries and more than 300,000 employees. On any given day, it is the world's wealthiest financial institution, depending on stock prices and currency rates.

Despite its ubiquity, however, HSBC operates very differently than most of its competitors. Here's why: HSBC has 8,500 offices worldwide. That's fewer than some of its rivals have in a single country. In many cities, for example, HSBC customers have to drive past six or seven branches of rivals banks to get to an HSBC office. Competitors are literally more convenient for customers, so HSBC must offer more value.

With the help of Cisco's IBSG organization, HSBC does this with one of the world's most advanced IT networks. Rather than invest in brick and mortar facilities, HSBC has put its money toward a powerful information and telecommunications network that gives it a speed and flexibility of which competitors can only dream. Because of this, customers are willing to drive past more conveniently located banks to seek out an HSBC office, where they believe they are better served.

To achieve this level of customer relevance, HSBC has devoted a great deal of resources to technology inside its operations and developed close ties to a handful of companies whose technology is relevant to it.

"We are unabashedly a technology-driven company," says Ken Harvey, Global Technology & Services Officer at HSBC. For example, fully one-third of the company's 300,000 workers serve in the HSBC Technology and Services (HTS) business unit, which spends $6 billion annually on IT. That's roughly 4 percent of revenue—at least twice, if not three times, what comparably-sized companies spend annually on IT.

The Cisco network deployed by HSBC is one of the world's largest privately owned networks. And given its capability, versatility, and dependability, HSBC literally runs its business on it. Today, the HSBC network carries everything from financial transactions to in-branch entertainment to digital signage information to Voice over IP (VoIP) phone calls to application services for the company. Because HSBC runs a single, converged network, it can offer competitive options that its rivals simply cannot. Take banking transactions, for example. Thanks to the Cisco network, HSBC can prioritize financial trades over other forms of network traffic, such as phone calls or even TelePresence. That capability might not sound much to a layman, but the millisecond advantage it provides translates to billions of dollars each year for HSBC customers. The HSBC platform is so powerful that company executives cite the network as one of the company's most powerful competitive advantages.

To say that Harvey's department is aligned with HSBC's broader business objectives would be an understatement. His organization, for example, has a goal of reducing unit-production costs 10 percent annually. This includes everything from withdrawing money from an ATM to processing a bill payment to completing an equity trade. HTS has accomplished the goal in six of the last seven years and is now pushing other business units to do the same. HTS gets to keep any cost reductions in excess of 10 percent to reinvest in new projects. Harvey, therefore, sees a clear and bidirectional relationship between operational excellence and innovation where each drives the other.

None of this would be possible had the company's business leaders not foreseen the business value of a world-class technology platform. Consider the bank's desire to be a more responsible global corporate citizen, for example. Thanks to advances in collaboration and video technology, HSBC was able to replace traditional, printed marketing materials with digital signage—sometimes even personalized digital signage. Not only does the network help the company reduce its carbon footprint, it also helps it provide a level of service that others do not.

In addition to personalized signage, for example, the Cisco network helps HSBC bring more expertise into every banking situation.

When a customer request goes beyond the capabilities of a local employee, for example, HSBC simply conferences in a virtual expert to provide video-based support. Experts can be instantly summoned to help anywhere around the world and in virtually any language. For example, HSBC employees can quickly collaborate on an individually tailored product for any customer and email it to the customer before he or she leaves the local branch.

The response has been phenomenal, says Harvey, for both customers, who enjoy better service, and for branch workers. HSBC doesn't have to train employees in 9,500 locations to be financial experts, just make them adept in how to use simple technology.

Because of its Internet-based business model, HSBC can expand into new markets more quickly than its competitors and ramp up to meet customers' needs. Take Vietnam and Pakistan, for example. Because of the bank's use of virtual financial experts and a network platform, it can expand its reach into these markets for less than what others spend on remodeling a local building. In 2007, HSBC began offering credit cards in several countries. The cost to HSBC? Less than $2 million.

"We moved into Vietnam and Pakistan just by expanding our reach through the network. No data centers, no operating centers, no new call centers—nothing. I don't need to build out that physical infrastructure, which is incredibly costly; everything is delivered through the network," says Harvey, who credits Cisco for showing the company how to become more relevant to its customers and excellent in its industry.

"There's only five suppliers that we really allow to use the word 'partner' with HSBC," says Harvey. "We spend $6 billion per year on technology, so a lot of people would probably like to be our partner. But Cisco is one of those few, where we really share a vision and we've done some neat things together."

What this means in business terms, going forward, is increased revenue, reduced complexity, lower operating costs, and higher customer satisfaction. That's relevance any business leader can understand. Combined with world-class execution, it's also excellence that rivals dread.

That not only goes for HSBC, but Cisco, too.

8

Michael Phelps *and* The Redeem Team
Superstar Performers and Winning Teams

"We're guaranteeing a gold medal. We're bringing it back."[1]

That's what 20-year old Carmelo Anthony predicted after a single practice with fellow members of the U.S. Olympic men's basketball team before the 2004 Summer Olympic Games.

Media analysts and basketball experts quickly dismissed Anthony's boast as little more than "youthful indiscretion" from a professional basketball player. But by the time the Olympic torch over Spiros Louis Stadium in Athens was extinguished a month later, his words hung in the air like a foul odor.

By then, the fourth installment of the Olympic Dream Team had become a nightmare. It lost three of eight games and finished with a disappointing bronze medal. The defeats were more than the total number of losses sustained by the U.S. team in all previous Olympics *combined*.

How could the one-time kings of the sport—the team that won 12 of the previous 14 gold medals—have fallen so far? It wasn't difficult to figure out.

Between the Sydney Olympics in 2000 and the games in Athens four years later, the rest of the world simply caught up to the United States in terms of strategy and skills and surpassed it in other areas. Shooting and passing—disciplines that Team USA traditionally dominated—had eroded precipitously by the time the team landed in Athens. In an embarrassing early-round, 92–73 loss to Puerto Rico,

Team USA shot just 3-for-24 from 3-point range and had nearly as many turnovers as field goals.[2] Afterward, *The New York Times* lamented, "The United States men's basketball team traveled all the way to Greece to find out they aren't even the best squad in their own neighborhood."[3]

Of all the shortcomings of Team USA, however, one stood out more than any other: teamwork. Lacking cohesion, the players worked more like individual freelancers than as a well-disciplined unit. They frequently wound up out of position on the court and misread assignments during the flow of games. Instead of following the script that their coaches suggested, players relied on the raw talent that made them superstars in the National Basketball Association (NBA). But those capabilities were simply no match for the well-coordinated team attacks unleashed on the Americans by Lithuania, Argentina, and, of course, Puerto Rico. The United States rallied in the bronze-medal game to avenge its early-round loss to Lithuania, but the win provided little solace.

More than attitude, most of the Americans simply lacked the skills and the understanding required to play *team* basketball. While the style doesn't feature the dazzling drives or signature dunks seen in the NBA, it does showcase a more unselfish play that leads to better shot selection, tougher defense, and improved rebounding. These were the very things that toppled Team USA in Athens and denied Anthony the gold he so confidently predicted.

Like Team USA in 2004, organizations that are dominated by superstars often encounter a loss of unity and purpose, leading to internal strife. Without shared organizational goals, employees focus more on their own glory than on organizational pursuits.

But the opposite scenario does not necessarily produce any better results. In an organization that values the *collective* without regard for the individual, creativity is stifled, new ideas are smothered, and groupthink prevails. This can limit an organization just as much as a lack of teamwork and prevent it from capturing new opportunities or foreseeing trouble ahead. And it may force high-performing individuals to leave.

That's precisely what Gary Burrell and Min Kao did after helping Allied Corporation develop pioneering navigation technology, leveraging the satellite-based global positioning system (GPS) developed by the United States government. Frustrated by their employer's reluctance to recognize the worth of their invention and pursue commercial applications for it, the two left and went on to form Garmin, now the world's largest manufacturer of consumer personal navigation devices.[4]

Stories such as these abound in the annals of companies big and small. Take the ad world. Thirty years ago, Dan Wieden and David Kennedy were young, brash, talented—and frustrated. Working for advertising giant McCann-Erickson (and later at the smaller firm of William Cain), the duo felt constrained and hemmed in as members of the agency's worldwide team. No matter how they tried, they couldn't persuade the account teams to push their clients to consider more creative print and broadcast advertising. So the two struck out on their own, along with a scrappy, up-and-coming Oregon shoe company that was looking to make a name for itself. That company was Nike. Not long after, Wieden came up Nike's most famous campaign: Just Do It.

McCann-Erickson could have had this glory, had it only listened to its bright young stars instead of depending on the opinion of the collective team.

What the examples of Team USA, Garmin, McCann-Erickson and others suggest is that instead of emphasizing individual achievement over teamwork or vice versa, organizations should do both. In this case, that means providing incentives and opportunities for individual superstars to shine while building a foundation for improved teamwork.

So how does an organization best do that?

It starts with performance metrics, incentive structures, and resource allocations that are geared toward individuals and teams. But it doesn't stop there. Organizational culture—measurable by few, but potent for all—plays a major role in determining the balance between individuals and teams.

How would your employees, for example, answer this question: "Will I become more successful pursuing my own ideas or working closely with a team?" The answer reveals a lot about your organization's mindset.

At Cisco, the answer is simple: "Yes"—you have to do both.

Cisco employees must excel at *both* individual responsibilities *and* team collaboration. Collaboration is not an excuse to pawn off responsibilities on team members or an opportunity to take credit for their work. Employees need to shine in their own light. At the same time, however, organizational objectives supersede individual achievements and goals.

This duality, of course, requires that Cisco encourage individual contributions and foster team performance.

Cisco evaluates individuals on how they challenge the status quo, disrupt existing businesses, and open their minds to new ideas, among other things. And Cisco's incentive structure reflects this philosophy. The company can reward superstars with bonuses that are not 10 or 20 percent more than that of the average employee, but double or triple that of the average employee.

Additionally, employees are measured on how they work across organizational boundaries and act in a selfless way to achieve shared goals. That includes both rank-and-file employees and senior executives. Cisco CEO John Chambers requires that in addition to individual excellence, candidates for senior executive promotions have made meaningful contributions to a cross-functional leadership team.

But how—and when—does the company use both individual superstars and collaborative teams? It depends on the situation.

Some initiatives require the passion, creativity, and quick thinking of a talented person. Others need the cross-functional expertise, complementary skill sets, and diverse resources of a team. As projects evolve over time, these requirements may sway one way or the other, so Cisco can adjust accordingly.

Consider Cisco's entry into the Sports & Entertainment business, for example. As recently as 2006, Cisco wasn't in this market in any meaningful way. That changed when one company dreamer fired up his Internet browser to kill some time.

StadiumVision: When Individual Superstars Dream Big

Each year at auto shows in Paris, New York, and Detroit, the world's leading automobile companies show off future vehicles known as concept cars. Designed to excite the buying public, these cars showcase the latest in design and technology.

Similarly, technology companies often develop prototype products that they, too, hope will excite buyers and stimulate developers. In many instances, they produce videos, white papers, and other materials to showcase the latest in their thinking.

One day while surfing Cisco's internal web site, company marketing manager Stuart Hamilton came across a video that stimulated his interest. The video showcased how networking technology could be applied to enhance the experiences of sports fans at ball parks and stadiums. The fans' infectious passion for sports and unbridled enthusiasm for technology struck a chord with Hamilton.

"That looks kind of cool," he said to himself.

The more he thought about the video, the more intrigued the long-time company veteran became. So he began searching for additional articles, PowerPoint presentations, press clippings—anything that contained information about Cisco's involvement with sports technology. Hoping to get additional insights, Hamilton tracked down Chief Demonstration Officer Jim Grubb, whose team produced the video. "How much of the video is real?" Hamilton asked.

"It's aspirational," he was told. "We need people to get behind it."

Hamilton sensed an opportunity. Knowing Cisco was concerned with over-promising and under-delivering on any idea, he put together what he calls an "unsolicited proposal for a job that didn't exist." The mission: serve as Cisco's chief investigator for sports and entertainment opportunities. Armed with little more than curiosity and enthusiasm, Hamilton began gathering information on sports technology.

With the blessing of then Cisco treasurer and avid sports fan Dave Holland, Hamilton started posing questions, not only to Cisco's thought leaders, but also to sports franchise owners around the world. "What would enhance fan experiences?" he asked. The ideas he collected ran the gamut from fan-friendly web sites to dedicated television stations to touch-screen interactive displays. Some of the ideas were compelling. A few were even theoretically possible. But none of them revolved around the equipment that Cisco actually made. So Hamilton turned his attention to Cisco technology and customer relevancy. And video seemed to be the answer.

Team owners, he discovered, were interested in putting wireless networking and Internet-enabled cameras throughout their stadium venues to provide fans exclusive video of on-field action and access to instant replays. They thought that would attract technologically-savvy fans who might otherwise stay home to watch sports on high-definition televisions. Hamilton thought that some of the ideas team owners envisioned were novel, but not really practical. He worried about fans at baseball games glancing down at their video-enabled mobile phones while a pop-up foul ball loomed over head. Instead, he formed an idea for something that appealed to their business sense. Why not, he proposed, use video technology to help sell more hotdogs, route stadium traffic, or promote upcoming events? On a May 2007 flight back to California after visiting yet another franchise owner, Hamilton sketched a proposal on the back of a napkin for a product that would later become known as Cisco StadiumVision.

Hamilton's idea called for the removal of the aging analog displays and televisions from stadiums and for the installation of new digital screens that could be programmed to address a myriad of needs. "Fans can upgrade seats at self-service kiosks and, using tablet PCs in the luxury suites, watch replays, check scores, answer sports trivia, order food or team merchandise, even check traffic before heading home," explained *Fast Company* magazine in 2010.[5] More than mere digital signage, StadiumVision is a programmable, networked solution that offers unprecedented flexibility and control over the content and distribution of information. Even teams with no money to spend on advanced technology liked the idea of using video inside their facilities to *generate* revenue.

After months of personal interviews, Hamilton was confident that his idea would sell. With no dedicated budget, no engineering staff, and no salespeople, he and a colleague looked to other sports-minded executives at the company for help.

"Let's see what you can do," they told him. So Hamilton pulled out his Visa card and called in some favors. He even traded some baseball tickets for lab space, software talent, and equipment. Soon, his ragtag team of conscripts and volunteers assembled a prototype of StadiumVision, cobbled together from Cisco routers and switches, digital signage screens, Unified Communications, and Scientific Atlanta video equipment. By August 2007, Hamilton began showing the prototype to any willing Cisco executive. They liked what they saw but asked tough questions. How many customers do you have? How many patents, marketing slogans, or ad ideas? The answer, of course, was zero.

In some companies—read *most*—that would have been the end of the line for Hamilton's dream. Without customer momentum or engineering support, ideas from left field have little chance of a thorough vetting, let alone long-term success. But not at Cisco.

Instead of watching his dream sink like a fly ball in center field, Hamilton worked with Holland and others to rally company-wide support around StadiumVision.

"In many companies, ideas that are generated outside of the traditional power structure never get off the ground because there is no mechanism to bring the right people together to evaluate it," says Holland. "We, however, have mechanisms in place that can make the most of ideas brought to us by advanced thinkers."

Because of the backing he received from management at the company, Hamilton confidently approached the NFL and proposed that Cisco showcase StadiumVision technology at the league's biggest venue: the Super Bowl. The league immediately turned him down. But Hamilton persisted. Based on a successful test in late 2007, the Arizona Cardinals gave the green light to display the technology on 30 video screens during the game—a very small opportunity at a very big event. Luckily for Cisco, Hamilton's StadiumVision idea debuted without a hitch, resulting in the technology's first customer.

Based on that success, Cisco's Sports & Entertainment business was off and running. Executives quickly lent engineers, marketing support, and even project managers—virtually everyone Hamilton needed to turn StadiumVision into a more commercially viable product. He, meanwhile, continued to make contacts that would turn into new business leads.

More than mere dollars, Cisco now realizes that the high-visibility sports businesses is a perfect showcase for its integrated video, mobility, and collaboration solutions. So the company has given Hamilton even more resources and support.

Since unveiling StadiumVision, Cisco has attracted a host of marquee customers, including some of the biggest names in the sports business. In 2008, for example, the New York Yankees signed a deal for 1,000 StadiumVision displays to be installed inside their new $1 billion baseball park. Then in the fall, the Dallas Cowboys football team signed on to put 3,000 screens inside their brand-new park. Other successes followed.

Thanks to broader support he received inside the company, Hamilton can solicit funds and secure immediate buy-in to his plans. He can also tap the expertise of thought leaders throughout the company and secure their commitments. More than anything, he can get visibility when he needs it and air cover when he doesn't. And he's not alone.

Throughout Cisco, star performers like Hamilton have helped the company in innumerable ways. That includes engineers, salespeople, managers, financiers, marketers, and others. Because Cisco gives them a great deal of latitude, they often lead the company to opportunities that it might have otherwise missed.

As invaluable as superstars are, however, an organization still needs its teams to amplify their work, scale initiatives, and drive cross-leverage between different functions. Key to building winning teams is cultivating an environment in which stars thrive but teamwork triumphs.

That's easier said than done, given the structural and cultural impediments present in many organizations. Until a few years ago, that included Cisco.

For instance, when Executive Vice President Rob Lloyd took over the North American sales organization in 2005, morale was high, and execution was thriving. He recognized that he had plenty of individual superstars but thought the organization could benefit from better teamwork—the kind he relied on as a youth playing hockey in Canada.

Lloyd joined Cisco in 1995 after creating one of the largest, independent computer dealerships in all of Western Canada. At its peak, Professional Computing Center of Calgary boasted $350 million in annual sales. When he joined Cisco, Lloyd hoped to merge the skills he picked up as a superstar entrepreneur with the lessons he learned as a team player on the hockey rink.

When Stars Align with Teams

Twenty-billion dollars in three years' time.

That's the audacious goal Lloyd set for Cisco's North American business in 2005. Just back from a successful three-year stint running Cisco's European operations, Lloyd was infused with confidence and eager to get started when he took over Cisco's largest region.

The timing couldn't have been better. Sales in the United States and Canada were growing quickly thanks to the rapidly expanding economy, and Cisco's product portfolio was brimming with new routers, switches, and video products, too. Because of these and other factors, customers were in a buying mood.

But $20 billion in annual sales by 2008? Even Lloyd's most trusted lieutenants thought that was a bit of a stretch—literally. At Cisco, ambitious objectives are often called "stretch goals" because the only way to achieve them is to extend oneself beyond what was once considered possible. When Lloyd arrived in 2005, Cisco's North American sales totaled $13.3 billion. As confident as they were, the men and women inside the North American sales organization didn't see any feasible way they could sustain the kind of growth required to reach $20 billion in annual sales in just three years. In fact, they were concerned that the law of large numbers would surely catch up to them one day. The absolute best they thought they could reach was $18 billion in annual sales—and even that was a stretch.

One reason for this skepticism was a lack of effective teamwork within the sales organization. Employees were simply more focused on individual accomplishments than on winning teams.

At this time, Cisco was solely organized around precisely defined geographies and product lines. There was little coordination between people working in different territories, even among those catering to a single customer who happened to have operations in multiple locales.

That was especially true of sales leaders, who enjoyed a great deal of direct authority and autonomy. The best of these individuals Cisco rewarded handsomely, so they stayed in front-line, customer-facing roles throughout their careers.

As a result, the company enjoyed consistent sales growth and high customer satisfaction but did not transfer field knowledge and customer intimacy between different parts of the company. This limited Cisco's ability to scale its expertise and prevented the company from capturing enough opportunities to attain Lloyd's $20 billion goal.

Lloyd believed that he could extract greater yields from individual superstars if he changed their roles. Instead of selling Cisco equipment and managing salespeople, he reassigned several of them to develop new solutions with individuals from other parts of the company. That had never been done before, but it was precisely what Lloyd thought the company needed.

When he began recruiting sales leaders to join his efforts, Lloyd encountered some initial pushback. Most liked their jobs and were wary of risking their careers on an unknown opportunity. In addition, they didn't like the idea of relinquishing direct authority over subordinates in favor of influencing people who did not report to them.

"When Rob approached me about the opportunity, I wasn't thrilled," says then-sales director Larry Payne. "From leading a sales organization to doing a crazy special project? I didn't know what it would mean for my career. I was told it was more visible and more important. But with no direct reports, I wasn't sure."

But Lloyd persisted. He promised Payne and other sales leaders that this would be good for their careers and beneficial to Cisco. He was not necessarily looking for sales leaders with market expertise, but for those who could build teams, identify opportunities, analyze data, foresee potential challenges, and collaborate effectively—all in the name of creating new deliverables that would help overcome the two-billion-dollar sales gap. He found these qualities not only in Payne, but also in Blake Sallé, a sales director in Washington, D.C, and nine other sales superstars from his organization.

In 2006, these leaders began to recruit their virtual teams. With no direct reports, they had to enlist the support of people throughout the company—many of whom they had never worked with before—to build their end-to-end solutions.

The teams first scanned for opportunities. Based on this, they generated hypotheses about how Cisco could make a greater impact in the markets. Then they did a deep analysis of customer buying habits, market trends, competitive threats, and the like. From there, they divided these opportunities into two categories: "just do its" and "figure it outs." The teams executed on the former and investigated the latter with pilot programs.

Based on the feedback from these programs, the teams drafted action plans, which were reviewed by Lloyd and his leadership team. With these plans, Cisco could move forward with end-to-end solutions in each vertical market.

Sallé's team, for example, was focused around increasing security revenue for Cisco. Detailed analysis revealed that the 80 percent of security customers who invested in just one product represented only 15 percent of product bookings. Conversely, just 3 percent of customers—those who purchased at least four products each—generated a whopping 61 percent of bookings. With this information in hand, Sallé's team drafted plans to refocus Cisco around a security architecture.

Another team was assembled to help increase channel sales. It brought together a dozen specialized systems engineers who devised a new program that scaled expertise. Their suggestion? Pull engineers from the field, where they spent a lot of their day solving problems for specific customers, and reassign them to jobs where they could combine their talents to create solutions that could be used by many customers over and over again.

This kind of teamwork was critical in devising new solutions. Payne, for example, had to learn the value of collaboration.

"Cisco is a very competitive, hard-driving sales culture. When Rob started talking collaboration, I thought it meant to play nice. But when I got into this role, I saw the real value. When you bring the right resources together, you get real results," says Payne.

And what were those results?

Thanks to their teamwork, Lloyd's organization reached $22.8 billion in annual sales in 2009—besting Lloyd's original goal by $2.8 billion, or 14 percent.

By getting his star players to apply their skills in new ways, Lloyd improved teamwork across his organization. In doing so, he saw the business grow by a whopping 71 percent. At the same time, his superstars saw their careers soar to new heights.

Sallé, for example, was promoted to vice president and asked to run worldwide sales for Cisco's Emerging Technologies Group. As for Payne, he earned a promotion, too. He's now vice president for State, Local, and Education sales for half of the United States.

This success could happen in your organization, too, if you nurture *both* teams *and* individuals.

For proof, look no further than the 2008 Beijing Olympic Games. While many remember the individual performances of superstar swimmer Michael Phelps, who won eight gold medals, Beijing was also the setting for the redemption of the United States basketball team.

Superstars and Teams: A Gold-Medal Combination

After returning from Greece with the bronze medal, USA Basketball went into overdrive to ensure that it would bring home the gold from Beijing in 2008. To inspire greater teamwork, officials turned to famed Duke University coach Mike Krzyzewski. A four-time national champion at the college level, Krzyzewski had a reputation for producing well-oiled teams. Krzyzewski's remedy was simple: "To me, teamwork is the beauty of our sport, where you have five acting as one. You become selfless."[6]

Getting superstars to check their egos at the door and enter a game in which they might not rack up many points or play as many minutes was a serious challenge. To accomplish this, Krzyzewski needed to find the right combination of players. Rather than simply gather the most recent NBA all-stars, he chose a group that could work together and leverage one another's skills. Once the team was assembled, Krzyzewski drilled them rigorously and coached them on their specific roles.

When the team took the court in Beijing, each player knew his duty and accepted his responsibility. No egos prevailed, and no *prima donnas* emerged. Take Jason Kidd, for example. Like all of his Team USA counterparts, Kidd is a superstar in his own right. The only player in NBA history to record at least 15,000 points, 7,000 rebounds, *and* 10,000 assists, he is a scoring, rebounding, and passing threat any night he takes the court. But in Beijing, Krzyzewski tasked Kidd with an unusual mission: help bigger, stronger players score by passing the ball to them. It was an unglamorous assignment for a nine-time NBA All-Star. But Kidd accepted his role with dignity and determination. In the entire tournament, he took just seven shots, but wound up dishing out 16 assists, including seven in a key semifinal victory over Argentina.

As a result of this kind of unselfish play, the "Redeem" Team took home the gold with an unblemished 8–0 record.

For one superstar in particular, the victories in Beijing were sweet redemption. Remember Carmelo Anthony, the young man who guaranteed the gold medal in 2004? As a member of Team USA in 2008, he was finally able to deliver on his promise and bring home the gold. "It was like night and day," Anthony said after Beijing. "It seemed like we were at the bottom in '04, and in '08 we were at the top."[7]

And the reason for the reversal of fortune? Teamwork, according to those who experienced it firsthand. After losing to Team USA in 2008, Spanish co-captain Pau Gasol summed up what he saw on the floor: "It's not that they're a lot better individually. As a team they're working better together."[8]

Superstar performers or winning teams? How about doing both?

9

West Point *and* Woodstock

Authoritative Leadership and
Democratic Decision Making

Rebel. Outlaw. Individualist.

Is there any company that embodies these images more than motorcycle manufacturer Harley-Davidson? Doubtful.

Since Marlon Brando challenged Harley-riding rivals in the film *The Wild One*, the company's bikes have represented freedom, non-conformity, and excitement to millions of enthusiasts around the world. From the unmistakable rumble of its V-twin engine to the counter-culture sneer of its stock symbol (HOG), Harley-Davidson has stood as an American icon for more than 100 years.

Despite the fearsome roar of its bikes, however, Harley-Davidson's management model once reflected a surprisingly New Age philosophy. "Beneath the image of a hard-riding, tough-as-nails Harley-Davidson bike is a company that thrives on the 'soft' side of management, emphasizing participation, inclusion, learning, and cooperation," noted *Fast Company* magazine in 1997.[1] Things didn't start off with such an egalitarian approach.

Harley-Davidson wouldn't be standing today had it not relied on a very strict, command-and-control management model to carry the company through some of its darkest days. In the early 1980s, the U.S. economy was slumping, and the motorcycle market was flooded with inexpensive Japanese imports. Harley-Davidson found itself drowning. In 1981, losses were mounting and market share was plummeting.

Knowing his company's survival was at stake, then-CEO Vaughn Beals moved swiftly. He reduced the workforce by 40 percent and extracted wage concessions of 9 percent from the remaining salaried workers. In addition, he told all employees to forget about raises for at least two years.

Though draconian in nature, these directives helped stabilize Harley-Davidson until the company could introduce new products—such as the popular Softail line—and persuade the government to impose tariffs on Japanese manufacturers. By 1986, the company's financial fortunes had improved.

Yet Harley-Davidson's long-term outlook remained uncertain. Company insiders knew they couldn't reduce costs much further or expect tariffs to compensate for shortcomings in manufacturing, distribution, and product design. Instead, Harley-Davidson needed ideas for making the company stronger. But where to find them wasn't readily clear. Even existing leaders sensed they were running out of inspiration.

In 1987, newly appointed president and chief operating officer Rich Teerlink wondered if the command-and-control model that had carried Harley-Davidson through the crisis of the early 1980s was meeting the company's long-term needs. "When an organization is under extreme pressure—so much so that one wrong move can mean its collapse—authoritarian leadership may very well be necessary," wrote Teerlink after retiring from the company in 2000. "[But] I knew we needed big changes in the motorcycle division. We had to identify some sort of strategy that could carry everyone forward—everyone meaning employees, customers, and all other stakeholders. We had to improve operations. And I felt strongly that we needed to change the way employees were being treated. They could no longer be privates, taking orders and operating within strict limits. We needed to continue to push, and push hard, to create a much more inclusive and collegial work atmosphere."[2]

Teerlink began to look for ways to drive decision making lower into the ranks of its employees. One of the things he did was to reach out to union workers and tell them they would play a role in helping to develop long-term company strategies. Then Teerlink pulled together teams of employees from different parts of the company, tasking them the big challenges of the day, including manufacturing defects and workforce morale.

Thanks to these and other changes, Harley-Davidson began to see improvements. By 1991, sales approached the $1 billion threshold for the first time. By the middle of the decade, orders outstripped supply—so much that Harley-Davidson had to expand its manufacturing capacity. With demand growing, the company's stock mounted an unrelenting upward climb.

Armed with new ideas and fresh perspectives, Harley-Davidson's leaders decided to eliminate altogether the hierarchical leadership pyramid and replace it with a more collaborative framework of overlapping "circles of leadership." These circles took responsibility for product development, sales, and support and were complemented by councils tasked with leadership and strategy. From an outside perspective, it wasn't exactly clear who did what at the company or who was in charge at any one moment. But insiders say the flexible framework provided an opportunity for more people to become involved in decision making. Soon, the circles were replicated throughout many parts of the company, and managers began singing the praises of the new model.[3]

The media and analyst communities were intrigued. A lovable management team produced bikes favored by Hells Angels? It was an irresistible attraction. A 1999 documentary for *PBS Television* profiled one Harley-Davidson plant in Kansas City where "natural work groups" oversaw production. The documentary described the facility as an "ideal workplace" where employees have "jobs of the future."[4]

For several, magical years, the HOG was riding high.

Then the landscape for motorcycles changed. The baby boomers and Rolex Riders that flocked to the brand in the early 2000s were approaching their sixties. Planning for retirement, not reliving *Easy Rider*, was foremost on their minds. With the economy beginning to turn, the lure of a $20,000 discretionary purchase began to wane for many would-be bike owners.

Unfortunately, Harley-Davidson's new-age management model was not optimized to handle the curves that lay ahead.

In 2007, for example, business got off to a rocky start after labor negotiations with workers at the York, Pennsylvania manufacturing facility broke down. Unable to reach an agreement after discussions, workers voted to strike. The company settled the strike within a few weeks, but the setback prompted it to lower financial expectations for the year.

Afterwards, Harley-Davidson couldn't seem to get in gear no matter how hard it tried. As the company began a gradual evolution back toward command-and-control leadership in the late 2000s,[5] it expressed optimism that sales would grow moderately. But in each year, they actually declined. Despite the best of intentions, Harley-Davidson was forced to trim its workforce—twice. By the end of 2009, a quarter of its workers were idle and management was looking for quick relief.[6] Barely a year after acquiring MV Agusta, a high-end European maker of motorcycles, Harley-Davidson announced in October 2009 that it would reverse course and sell the company.[7]

How did things get so bad? As far back as a decade ago, there were signs that Harley-Davidson was beginning to operate with less speed. Former IT director Cory Mason summed up what many insiders had come to believe about the decentralized model: "In some respects, it's slower because you have to bring all the stakeholders together."[8] The experience of Harley-Davidson begs the question of whether a company is better off with a command-and-control management model or with one that is more egalitarian. Harley-Davidson tried one, switched to the other, and is now switching back. Each, of course, comes with advantages and drawbacks.

Command-and-control models are typically patterned after military hierarchies studied at the top military academies around the world including Saint-Cyr in Coëtquidan, France, and the U.S. Military Academy in West Point, New York. Instead of generals, colonels, majors, captains, and lieutenants, however, businesses have senior vice presidents, vice presidents, directors, and so on. Power flows downward through a hierarchal pyramid of authority. Such centralized models provide scale, replicability, and accountability. Business leaders can be assured that their orders will be followed accurately and according to a clearly defined set of metrics. The downside to this type of model, however, is that it is not optimized for speed or flexibility. In top-down organizations, thought leadership is typically limited to a small few, and new ideas are often eschewed in favor of the status quo.

In contrast, collaborative environments that drive decision making deeper into an organization often foster creativity and operate with greater speed. In such decentralized environments, workers from all ranks are valued, not just for their labor, but their ideas, too. The beauty of such organizations is the ability to draw from a wide variety of inputs, without relying on a single person for approval on every decision. In many instances—from open source software to the famed Woodstock concert event of 1969—loose hierarchies, while unconventional, can produce extraordinary things. But these bottom-up models often suffer from an inability to execute decisively or measure progress accurately.

Scale or speed? Replicability or flexibility?

Over the years, companies have generally picked one model *or* the other. But in doing so, they cut themselves off from the benefits that the alternative provides. To combat this, some organizations, such as Harley-Davidson, change models as economic or market conditions warrant. But timing a management model to a specific set of environmental circumstances is risky at best.

What if you didn't have to choose between top-down, centralized authority and decentralized decision making?

Maybe, the answer is to do both.

Cisco, the Early Years: Taking Orders, Following Directions

In its early years, Cisco did not always follow the principle of doing both. The company was originally governed by a traditional, centralized management model. For the most part, this served the company well, especially during the heady years of the 1990s.

With millions and then billions of dollars of revenue pouring into the company, and thousands of new employees joining it, Cisco needed to keep a tight reign over its operations. Among other things, the command-and-control model helped Cisco manage its growth and ensured company leaders could count on their initiatives to be executed quickly and efficiently. And they could measure how these decisions succeeded or failed.

In addition, this model disciplined leaders to view every decision through the lens of scalability. The question they often asked their lieutenants was, "Will it scale?" If the answer was "No," then employees were pressed to focus their energies on things that would.

While this enabled Cisco to keep up with demand for its core products, it made the company more rigid and less accepting of alternative ideas.

That included input from some of its own veterans. "For a super-capitalist company, it ran more like a centralized, planned economy," says Bob Agee, a former vice president who joined Cisco in 1997 to run operations in Russia and the Commonwealth of Independent States. "When I was 22-years-old working on my own as a young country GM in Nigeria for Xerox, I had more autonomy than I did as a Cisco vice president."

The company's reluctance to look at things differently also made it difficult for Cisco to foresee new opportunities or potential calamities. Never was that more apparent than when the bottom on the market for telecommunications equipment and services collapsed in 2001.

Within a few short months, Cisco's sales fell by half, and the company was stuck with $2 billion worth of inventory it could not sell. In a painful decision, the company was ultimately forced to cut 12 percent of its regular employees.

Afterward, CEO John Chambers began to wonder if the company's reliance on a single management model was a major part of the problem. Command-and-control served the company well in so many ways. But it didn't enable the company to pursue more than three or four corporate priorities each year. And it didn't allow Chambers to leverage the on-the-ground knowledge of his business leaders to the fullest extent possible.

Would it help to drive decision making deeper into the company and open it up to a large number of managers? More and more Chambers began to believe so. He knew he had plenty of people who could make decisions, and he was confident that having more minds focused on more opportunities would bring about better resolutions to business challenges.

The more Chambers thought about the idea, the more he became convinced that the ideal corporate structure wasn't a choice between command-and-control *or* decentralized decision making, but a judicious blend of *both*.

By blending the best of both models, Chambers reasoned, Cisco could better anticipate opportunities and prepare for challenges, rather than merely reacting to them.

Power to the People: Inside Cisco's Councils and Boards

To get more company leaders more involved in decision making, Chambers started shifting certain powers from the company's traditional business owners—think heads of sales, marketing, manufacturing, and engineering—to newly-formed teams populated with managers from various parts of the company. Known as councils and boards, these teams complement the company's more traditional hierarchy, providing the scale and replicability of a centralized company *and* the speed and flexibility of a decentralized one.

Unlike informal company committees, Cisco's councils and boards have very specific missions and duties.

Councils form around opportunities that have the potential to drive $10 billion in annual revenue within 3 to 5 years. Today, the company has nine councils: five focused on customer segments, two on innovation, and two on operational excellence. Councils set the long-term direction for their respective segment or area, championing investments and go-to-market priorities. Each council is responsible for its business segment or specific cross-segment goal.

For instance, you may remember the Emerging Countries Council, which was discussed in Chapter 6, "The Beaten Path *and* The Road Less Traveled." That council helped double Cisco's business in emerging countries between 2006 and 2008.

What makes the councils unique is that they are populated with—and led by—cross-functional teams of senior executives who are empowered to make critical business decisions "at the table." Each council is composed of executives representing a range of functions, such as sales, finance, operations, IT, and marketing. Each member has the authority to approve or disapprove plans without having to check with a boss. Because of this, decisions about entering new markets, making acquisitions, and reallocating resources now move quickly and effectively.

Not surprisingly, council leadership is among the most sought-after assignments in the company. To ensure that each council has the right cross-functional composition, Chambers is personally involved in selecting leaders and members.

In addition to the councils, there are more than two dozen active boards that report to the councils and align to Cisco's ever-expanding list of priorities. Boards form around market opportunities that can drive $1 billion in annual revenue within 3 to 5 years.

For example, Cisco scaled Stuart Hamilton's sports and entertainment initiative with a newly created board. Leveraging Hamilton's early successes, the board garnered more resources than Hamilton alone could secure, providing a foundation that allowed Cisco to capture new opportunities. The board is now engaged with more than two dozen major stadium and team owners and is building a potential billion-dollar business.

Cisco has also formed boards around China, sustainability, advertising, and smart power grids. After major goals have been reached, boards are disbanded, and their duties transferred to traditional functions inside the company.

And members are not just senior executives. The boards and councils also commission small working groups of employees to come together, solve a particular problem, and quickly disband.

The beauty of the boards and councils is that they do not operate independent of Cisco's traditional hierarchy. Instead, the two work together. This dual structure is designed to provide Cisco the efficiency of a top-down company with the customer intimacy and responsiveness of a decentralized one (see Figure 9.1).

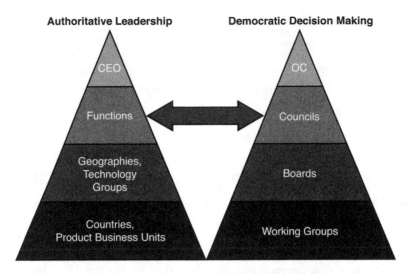

Figure 9.1   Authoritative leadership and democratic decision making

"At Cisco, the traditional organizational structure is no longer the primary lever for getting work done," says Brian Schipper, senior vice president of human resources. "We maintain traditional leadership roles, but we complement them with teams of people who can make decisions horizontally across the organization, resulting in a significant acceleration of work."

Of course, not everyone is convinced.

Since Cisco introduced its councils and boards, scores of analysts, journalists, and other company watchers have questioned the wisdom of the model. "Management by committee," some say. "Corporate socialism," others have mused. Some have even wondered if Cisco is practicing "matrix management in disguise."

None of these is accurate. Take matrix management, for example. While matrix models have certain benefits, they have been inadequate when it comes to improving cross-functional effectiveness. In a matrix organization, employees tend to defend their functional resources and focus on functional duties. Conversely, Cisco councils emphasize collaboration and teamwork. They start with a shared goal and then devise a workable strategy with which to achieve it (see Table 9.1).

TABLE 9.1   Councils and Boards Versus Matrix Management

Matrix Management	Councils and Boards
Decisions degenerate to lowest common denominator.	Decisions formed around highest possible aspiration.
Siloed goals drive competition between functions or divisions.	One corporate-wide P&L drives shared goals.
Resources hoarded for functional or divisional benefit.	Resources shared for the greater corporate good.
Participants need to get decisions approved within their function or division.	Participants are empowered to make decisions—at the table—on behalf of their functions.

The critiques come as no surprise to Cisco, which has been adapting the model since it was first unveiled in 2002. In fact, the company did not see strong results from the first generation of councils partially because executives were not particularly enthusiastic about participating. They had more allegiance to their parent organizations than to the councils and were not empowered to do anything but make recommendations for solving cross-functional problems.

While the councils originally served as mere obstacle removers, they soon began to set the strategy and drive initiatives for their respective areas. Today, councils are accountable for revenue growth, profit contribution, customer satisfaction, and market share in their customer segments, while the traditional business functions maintain responsibility for their own functional areas.

But councils do more than deliver numbers for the company. They also serve as a way to develop future leaders.

"What we try to do is get individuals working on councils and boards to move out of their areas of expertise and rely less on functional knowledge and more on leadership skills," says Randy Pond, executive vice president of operations, processes, and systems.

"When they have shared goals before them, we are best able to leverage their individual experiences, ideas and disciplines."[9]

Take Executive Vice President Sue Bostrom, for example. She not only leads Cisco's marketing organization, but also co-leads the Small Business Council. Similarly, Chief Technology Officer Padmasree Warrior co-leads the Connected Architecture Council, while Chief Information Officer Rebecca Jacoby serves on the Enterprise Business Council.

So how does a company empower employees *and* ensure that they follow management's expectations? That is a tricky challenge for any company, let alone one that is trying to extend decision-making authority to as many as 3,000 leaders. Implementing the dual management model was necessary, but it was not sufficient. Recognizing the enormity of the challenge, Cisco devised an additional mechanism to get its people aligned, moving in the same direction and speaking the same language.

Here's how.

One Cisco, One Page: How Discipline Improved Alignment

At various times throughout its history, Cisco has navigated around certain plateaus that have stymied other companies. Think sales thresholds, market expansions, and acquisitions. In doing so, Cisco has had to refine strategy and execution plans on an ongoing basis. But the challenge associated with this effort has frustrated company leaders on occasion. Why was it sometimes so difficult to align strategy and execution and at other times, so painless?

Leaders eventually discovered that different parts of the company used different terminology, tools, and mechanisms for discussing opportunities and measuring outcomes. When consistency and discipline were missing, confusion and misunderstanding often filled the void. In other words, Cisco had a basic process and language problem.

"If we get our people speaking the same language and using the same measures of accountability, would our strategy and execution both improve? Would our collaboration increase?" many wondered. The questions led to the creation of a new discussion framework that Cisco began to use internally. It revolved around three simple words: vision, strategy, and execution.

To eliminate any ambiguity, Cisco attached a very precise meaning to each word so it would trigger behaviors universally understood throughout the company. Specifically, Cisco defined "vision," "strategy," and "execution" as follows:

- **Vision**—A 3- to 5-year value proposition Cisco will deliver to customers, based on market transitions. It answers a simple question: What is the end result we want to accomplish? Its time horizon is typically 5 years or more.
- **Strategy**—The key attributes and actions that sustain Cisco's differentiation over multiple generations of products and services. Its time horizon is typically over the next 2 to 4 years.
- **Execution**—A series of activities that Cisco will undertake and measure over the next 12 to 18 months to carry out the objectives behind a strategy.

In essence, V, S, and E can be simplified to: Where Are We Headed; How Will We Get There; and What Are We Doing? In practical terms, the Operating Committee sets the company vision, the councils define the strategy, and the functions execute.

"The vision drives agreement, the strategy fosters alignment, and the execution promotes accountability. It's not just taxonomy. It's actually a tool for getting employees to lay out a plan in terms that everyone can understand and to which they can execute," according to Cisco Vice President Ron Ricci, a key champion of the approach (see Table 9.2).

TABLE 9.2   VSE Drives Agreement, Alignment, and Accountability

	Vision	Strategy	Execution
End Result	Agreement	Alignment	Accountability
Underlying Basis	Market Transitions	Sustainable Differentiation	Measurable Results
Time Horizon	5+ years	2–4 years	12–18 months

Since unveiling the VSE framework, Cisco has found that it can move with greater consistency, which has helped Cisco operate with agility to take advantage of market transitions that come about by changing business conditions or technological breakthroughs. Take the consumer market, which Cisco has entered with high expectations.

In 2010, for example, consumers in the United States alone are expected to spend upwards of $165 billion on consumer electronics—everything from mobile phones to flat screen televisions to digital recorders to home networking products and more.[10] That's 63 percent more than they spent in 2004.[11]

Until recently, Cisco had captured only a fraction of the annual spending. One reason: the company's ad hoc approach to the market. Prior to developing the consumer VSE, various business units were trying to serve different parts of the market independent of one another. Cisco's service provider group, for example, developed cable set-top boxes for home users, while Cisco's Linksys group sold point products to consumers through retailers without leveraging the broader Cisco sales machine. Then there was the company's media solutions group, which was building platforms for social networking, content targeting, and site administration all by itself. Instead of cross-functional decision making and execution, different groups operated in isolated silos. This was exemplified by Cisco's initial consumer marketing approach, which was little more than a house of brands that bore little resemblance to the "Cisco" name.

Without an integrated vision or strategy, many inside and outside of the company struggled to understand why Cisco was in the consumer business at all. The low-margin, high-volume consumer business model seemed at odds with Cisco's core business model, which revolved around catering to big-ticket business customers who paid top dollar for equipment in return for world-class engineering and unrivaled support. In contrast, the consumer market prized rapid innovation above all else—except, perhaps, for competitive prices.

To provide clarity to outsiders and insiders alike, Cisco's Consumer Business Council rigorously applied the VSE framework to everything that it was doing in the consumer market. That included everything from the products it developed to the partners it engaged to the branding policies that it pursued.

To develop its vision, the company zeroed in on three macro trends: the rise of the empowered user, the increased connectivity of consumer devices, and the growing use of video. More than simple evolutions, these market transitions represented some of the biggest changes yet in telecommunications, consumer electronics, and computing. Take the rise of the empowered end user, for example.

"When I started at Cisco, we would innovate at the enterprise level and then drive out our investments into R&D for the mass market," says Ken Wirt, vice president of consumer marketing. "Now the investment paradigm has been flipped on its head. Today, innovation starts at the consumer level, and makes its way back into the enterprise." One example of this is the way the new generation of workers ushered into the workplace collaborative technologies like Facebook, Twitter, and instant messaging. Rather than wait for IT managers to deploy these tools in a traditional top-down, enterprise-wide fashion, younger workers simply started using them in their jobs. This trend represents a fundamental shift in the way that enterprises acquire and use technology, and in the way that workers collaborate.

More than just in the workplace, empowered users are exercising influence in far greater ways, including how products are designed, manufactured, and brought to market. More and more, they are demanding ubiquitous connectivity in consumer devices so they can communicate anytime, anywhere, and on any device. This has led to the introduction of a variety of connected devices—everything from personal computers to digital video recorders to MP3 players. That's quite a change from just a few years ago when only your mobile phone and your computer connected to a network. Today, almost everything in your briefcase and your child's backpack connects. If it has a chip or a plug, chances are it is online.

And what are people doing with their networks? Putting more video on it. Take YouTube: Every minute, 20 hours of video is uploaded to the popular video hosting and viewing site. Every day, hundreds of thousands of new videos are uploaded, according to the company.[12] With these trends in mind, Cisco articulated its consumer vision: "Enabling people to live a connected life that is more personal, more social, and more visual."

This vision, you might notice, directly addresses each of the three major market transitions. *Personal* refers to the empowered user. *Social* focuses on connectivity. And *visual*, of course, rallies the team around video.

Just as the three transitions formed Cisco's vision, the link *between* them soon formed the crux of Cisco's strategy: "Leverage the network as the platform to deliver the next generation of consumer video experiences—integrating devices, software, and the Internet." The latter—the architectural integration of the devices and the leveraging of network—was key to the company because it formed the foundation for its sustainable differentiation going forward.

Cisco's push into consumer markets has yielded substantial gains. Consumer sales are robust, relevance with media companies is increasing, and Cisco's influence in video continues to rise. There are more than 200 million Cisco devices in homes today.

To long-time company veterans including Senior Vice President Ned Hooper, who leads the consumer business for Cisco, the impact of the consumer VSE cannot be overstated. "The vision made us agree on a common destination, and the strategy gave us focus. The execution, meantime, helps us prioritize. Thanks to this, we've combined devices and software over the Internet to create new experiences," he says. "You can only do that if the whole company comes together."

What a Difference a Decade Makes

When the technology bubble burst in 2001, Cisco was ill-prepared for what followed. Given the company's centralized management model, all it could do was react to external forces.

Contrast that with the economic freefall of 2008 and 2009. Thanks to the dual management model, Cisco was better able to navigate its way through an economic downturn than ever before.

When Cisco realized that orders were slowing and an economic downturn was imminent, the company's command-and-control leadership model kicked into high gear. Within weeks, executives identified $1.4 billion worth of discretionary spending that they could target for elimination. Because of the authority they wielded, they were certain that their directives to eliminate travel, cut back on the use of outside contractors, and even to raise cafeteria prices would be followed. And they were—immediately.

That was the easy part.

The hard part was identifying which projects to eliminate and which to prioritize. That's where the councils stepped in. Thanks to their more hands-on knowledge of intimate details deep within the company, councils and boards identified an additional $500 million that could be put to better use. And they did so within just three months.

Take the Enterprise Business Council (EBC), which focuses on opportunities with large, corporate customers. After reevaluating priorities in light of the slowdown, the EBC decided to concentrate investment resources on several of Cisco's most strategic customers. By better meeting their business and technology needs, the council helped drive a 15 percent jump in product sales and a whopping 131 percent spike in services sales within these accounts.

Thanks to doing both—a centralized model that maintained a tight reign on expenses *and* a collaborative model that zeroed in on new opportunities while reprioritizing initiatives—Cisco avoided the wholesale layoffs that plagued many technology companies in 2008 and 2009.

While others were hitting the brakes, Cisco was revving the accelerator. During a single quarter in 2009 alone, it made four acquisitions.

"When you do four acquisitions in a quarter—two of them multibillion dollar—you really do have to have your teams moving in a couple of directions. And you have to coordinate them. That's a perfect example of how [Cisco has] been utilizing cross-functional teams," said Catharine Trebnick, a senior analyst at Avian Securities.[13]

Another benefit of the dual management model? The company still scales. By increasing the number of decision makers inside the company, Cisco has been able to expand its list of annual priorities from a mere handful per year to several dozen at once. In 2010, for example, the company boldly set out to purse two dozen new markets.

And the result of all these benefits: With its blend of authoritative leadership *and* democratic decision making, Cisco can run like a finely-tuned Harley rumbling down the highway.

10

The Journey Begins

Breakthrough products. New revenue streams. Higher performing teams.

You've read how applying the concept of "doing both" helped Cisco produce these gains and more. But what about your organization: Can doing both propel it, too?

I believe it can—and in virtually every aspect of your business. That includes product development, partner relations, market expansion, executive leadership, and more. Among other benefits, doing both can help an organization speed its decision-making, scale its expertise, replicate its successes, and operate more flexibly.

But where to begin, you may wonder?

One intuitive place to start is with a current challenge or opportunity. Perhaps you want to enter an adjacent market that offers substantial growth potential but lower margins. Perhaps you struggle to balance your investments between innovation and operational excellence. Should you do this or that? Undoubtedly, you are analyzing the potential outcomes of various decisions, possibly drawing up lists of pros and cons for each. This exercise, of course, can be exhausting. It often leads to fractious disagreements, unfortunate trade-offs, and lingering resentments that can build if left unchecked.

Is this really an optimal approach?

Cisco's breakthrough occurred when its leadership team realized that choosing one thing over another was often a false choice. Take business partners, for example. Though it seems incomprehensible now, Cisco didn't always reward them as well as it does today. Because it has always focused on satisfying customers, Cisco paid less attention to devising strategies and implementing policies that recognized its partners. As a result, partner satisfaction suffered. When that happened, Cisco found itself in a world of hurt trying to restart its business after the dot-com meltdown of 2001. Only after committing to doing both—satisfying customers and gratifying partners—did its fortunes improve.

The same occurred when the company learned to do disruptive and sustaining innovation simultaneously. The former helps Cisco create fast-growing markets while the latter helps drive its high-margin businesses. Together, they deliver both growth and profitability.

Cisco has embraced this ideal in many other areas of its business. The more it does, the more doing both becomes steeped in the company's culture. Doing both therefore acts as a force multiplier, where its impact in one area magnifies its impact in another. The councils that complement Cisco's traditional leadership model, for example, have proven critical to the company's efforts to expand into emerging countries, pursue new technologies, and elevate the work of top performers.

For this reason and so many others, Cisco is more likely to do both when faced with a challenge or decision.

But it's not easy. Take new business models. Their very introduction will likely threaten not only your people, but many of your processes as well. They will challenge your financial underpinnings and possibly alter your go-to-market strategy. But they are absolutely critical if you wish to engage new customers and diversify your offerings.

So why don't more people do both?

Allegiance to the status quo is often the answer. Undoubtedly, you have heard the excuses: "If it isn't broken, don't fix it." "Stick to your knitting." While these home-spun witticisms seem perfectly reasonable, they may be a cover to avoid doing something new or different.

You might not notice when this is happening. Reluctant to overhaul your operations now and then? That will leave you vulnerable to sudden shifts in the economy and unprepared for market transitions. Preoccupied with perfecting your products? That could distract you from addressing your customers' critical needs.

But you can avoid these tradeoffs by doing both. Whether your organization develops technology for a global market or provides a service for a local audience, the benefits of doing both still apply.

If you are in the healthcare industry, you can improve patient care *and* reduce costs. If you're in manufacturing, you can increase productivity *and* lower greenhouse emissions. And if you're in the public sector, you can expand access to information *and* protect the privacy of your constituents.

In almost every scenario, Cisco believes the best approach is to do both—and not just in product development, but in employee relations, customer service, partner management, and more.

That's as true today as it was nearly 75 years ago when the builders of the Golden Gate Bridge joined hundreds of thousands of gawkers, engineering enthusiasts, and wide-eyed dreamers in the inaugural walk across the 6,700-foot long span. That momentous occasion would never have been possible had the people behind the bridge not embraced the concept of doing both in the bridge design.

To overcome the objections of a wary public, chief engineer Joseph Strauss had to propose a design that would not ruin the natural splendor of the San Francisco Bay. But he also knew the Golden Gate Bridge—then the longest span in the world—needed to be sturdy. Because he recognized that he could only succeed by doing both—endowing the bridge with strength *and* beauty, Strauss and his colleagues prevailed. The bridge turned out to be not only one of the world's most enduring jewels, but also one of its greatest feats of engineering.

If doing both could span the Golden Gate and connect Cisco to millions around the world, imagine what it can do for you.

Epilogue

Doing both works in business.

I believe it applies even more broadly—and naturally—in life.

As I reflect on my own life, it occurs to me how often I use doing both to overcome a challenge or to seize an opportunity. And not just as a professional in the technology industry, but as a father, son, husband, neighbor, and citizen, too.

Millions of us strive to achieve at the office and succeed at home. We try to live for today and plan for tomorrow. We labor long and hard to provide our children the very things that our parents gave to us—roots to keep them grounded and wings to help them soar.

A son in the East and a father in the West, I aim to respect tradition and to embrace progress. I endeavor to fulfill my emotional needs and nurture my intellect. I work to be tough when the moment demands and compassionate when the need arises.

But while there are unlimited opportunities to do both, one example has served me more than any other: preparing meticulously *and* improvising enthusiastically.

This is something I first learned as a 15-year-old applying to the Indian Institute of Technology (IIT). Then, I was one of approximately 150,000 applicants—a long shot considering the university accepted just 1,500 students each year.

Given these odds, I wondered how best to prepare for the university's entrance exams. I had heard about a preparatory class in

Delhi, but that was six hours from my home and, moreover, a world away from the small-town life I knew. In all my life, I had never been to a big city. The thought of visiting one, let alone living there, was daunting. To me, a big town was one with more than two movie theaters. Delhi had somewhere north of 60—an unimaginable number to me.

Still, I wanted to attend the class. But there were hurdles to overcome. For starters, I had no place to sleep. My family couldn't afford an apartment or hotel, and we knew no one with whom I could stay. Furthermore, the four-month course was already more than half over when I learned of it. Ever persistent, I asked my father to make some inquiries. As luck would have it, a colleague told him that there might be a place for me at a nearby army base. "Send him over and we'll see what we can do," he said.

Uncertain of what to expect, I boarded the bus and headed for Delhi. This was a bit out of character, to say the least. My life to that point had been geared around studies and family life. There were routines and rhythms that I practiced over and over. They became my touchstones. A perfectionist by nature, I didn't generally like to leave things to chance or doubt. And yet, the situation compelled me to step out of my comfort zone.

When I arrived in Delhi, I found there was no bed for me at the army base, no desk to use for studies, and no place to store my clothes. Instead, I was pointed to a veranda without walls. Where will I eat, I wondered? What if someone steals my things, I asked? Don't worry, I was told. Make the best of your situation and see what happens. And so I did.

I made a pillow from books and clothes, and fashioned a desk with a light that I made from a single bulb and a few wires pulled from a nearby electrical socket. For seven weeks, the outdoor porch was my humble home. Every night I would return from class late to find a plate of food set out for me by my makeshift bed. Though the food was cold, it warmed my heart and fueled my desire.

Doing both—preparing and improvising—paid off. My entrance exam scores won me acceptance to a prestigious program at IIT, which changed the trajectory of my life completely. Gaining entry to that school opened the door for me to come to America, where I continued to do both.

That includes the time, some years later, when I needed to secure a summer internship during my MBA program at The Wharton School of Business. The year was 1990—a tough year in terms of economic prosperity and job growth.

Though I couldn't do anything about the economy, I was determined to land the best job possible. One of the firms I set my sights on was Bain & Company. With a roster of clients that included many of the world's top companies, Bain was one of the world's premier management consulting organizations. It was a dream destination for many of us at Wharton. But getting in wasn't easy.

To hook up with Bain, students had to work through the campus placement center and hopefully qualify for an interview when the company came to town. Bain offered first-round, on-campus interviews to 225 students from Wharton's pool of 750. Only 15 of these would be invited for a second-round interview in Boston. And Bain planned to hire just two interns.

While the odds of being hired weren't good, I was hopeful nonetheless. Call it hubris or naïveté, but I honestly thought that having a degree from one of India's finest engineering schools and top grades from Wharton, along with strong work experience, would distinguish me from other candidates. But it didn't. When Bain posted the names of the 225 students it wanted to interview, my name wasn't on the list. My best shot at getting hired with one of the top companies in management consulting was over before it started.

Or was it?

Remembering the times in my life when I refused to let a setback stop me, I decided not to take no for an answer. Yes, I had the scores and grades required. I had the smarts and knowledge, too. But while I had done everything in my power to prepare for getting a position with Bain, I hadn't yet improvised when the moment demanded.

So I rang Bain and asked that its recruiters give me additional consideration. No, I was firmly told: "We have our procedures, and we follow them."

Undaunted, I showed up at the hotel where interviews were underway. "Just give me five minutes," I said. Once again, I was told that there would be no time for me. Refusing to give up, even if it meant embarrassing myself in front of my classmates and a potential employer, I sought out the top recruiter and asked if he would chat with me between interviews. "My calendar is full, and there's simply no time in the day for that," he said.

Despite being told "no" several times, I waited outside the interviewer's room all day and made small talk whenever an opportunity presented itself. After his final meeting of the day, he emerged in a hurry and apologized one last time but said he had to take a cab to the airport. "Let me ride with you," I pleaded. "We can talk on the way."

Exhausted, the interviewer relented.

I don't remember what I said exactly, but I must have left an impression. When the list of the 15 finalists was posted, my name was finally on it. Better still, after the last round of interviews in Boston, I was one of the two people offered a job. That wouldn't have happened without *both* preparing *and* improvising.

Doing both had again paid off. Without it, I wouldn't have the story that I do today.

Thanks for allowing me to share it.

About the Author

Inder Sidhu is Senior Vice President of Strategy and Planning for Worldwide Operations at Cisco, the $40 billion worldwide leader in networking for the Internet. A member of the company's Operating Committee, Inder also co-leads Cisco's Emerging Countries Council, which drives business success in fast-growing geographies like China, India, Brazil, Mexico, and the Middle East.

From 2006 to 2009, Inder co-led the Enterprise Business Council, which is responsible for Cisco's corporate business, representing about half of the company's total revenue.

Since joining Cisco in 1995, Inder has served in executive leadership positions in the Sales, Services, and Business Development organizations. He was the VP/GM Worldwide Professional Services, VP/GM Advanced Engineering Services, and VP Strategy and Business Development, Customer Advocacy.

Inder was previously with McKinsey & Company, an international management consulting company. He has also worked at Intel and Novell.

Inder is a graduate of the Advanced Management Program at Harvard Business School and holds an MBA from the Wharton School of Business of the University of Pennsylvania. He also holds a Master's degree in Electrical and Computer Engineering from the University of Massachusetts, Amherst, and a Bachelor's degree in Electrical Engineering from the Indian Institute of Technology, Delhi, India.

Inder channels his passion for education into guest lecturing at Harvard Business School, Stanford University, and the Haas School of Business at the University of California-Berkeley. He also serves on the Board of Directors of Goodwill of Silicon Valley.

Inder lives in Saratoga, California, with his wife and three children.

Endnotes

Chapter 1

[1] James Wilkins, Editorial, *San Francisco Call Bulletin* (August 1916); in Kevin Star, *Endangered Dreams: The Great Depression in California* (New York, NY: Oxford University Press, 1997), 329.

[2] Henry Petroski, "Art and Iron and Steel," *American Scientist* (July/August 2002), http://www.americanscientist.org/issues/feature/art-and-iron-and-steel/5 (accessed January 20, 2010).

[3] "American Experience: Golden Gate Bridge," *PBS Online (KQED)* (April 16, 2004), http://www.pbs.org/wgbh/amex/goldengate/peopleevents/ (accessed November 13, 2009).

[4] American Institute of Architects, "America's Favorite Architecture," *Favorite Architecture*, http://favoritearchitecture.org/afa150.php (accessed November 13, 2009).

[5] "Seven Wonders of the Modern World," *American Society of Civil Engineers* (1994), http://www.asce.org/history/seven_wonders.cfm#ggb (accessed November 13, 2009).

[6] John B. McGloin, "Symphonies in Steel: Bay Bridge and the Golden Gate," *Virtual Museum of the City of San Francisco*, http://www.sfmuseum.net/hist9/mcgloin.html.

[7] Jim Collins and Jerry I. Porras, *Built to Last: Successful Habits of Visionary Companies*, 1994, 45: HarperCollins Publishers, New York, NY. Copyright © 1994 by Jim Collins and Jerry I. Porras. Reprinted with permission from Jim Collins.

[8] "Interbrand Best Global Brands List 2009," Interbrand Corporation, http://www.interbrand.com/best_global_brands.aspx (accessed November 12, 2009).

Chapter 2

[1] "Textile Washing Products: Global Industry Guide." *MarketResearch.com* (February 2009), http://www.marketresearch.com/product/display.asp?productid=2104548.

[2] Procter & Gamble, "2008 Annual Report," 2.

[3] Ibid.

[4] From *The Innovator's Dilemma: When New Technologies Cause Great Firms to Fail* by Clayton Christensen, Harvard Business Press, 1997. Excerpt reprinted with permission of Harvard Business Press.

[5] Tom Krazit, "Google Looks to Fast-Track Employee Ideas," *CNET* (June 18, 2009), http://news.cnet.com/8301-1023_3-10267848-93.html.

[6] Iomega, "2000 Annual Report," 15.

[7] Iomega, "2001 Annual Report," 3.

[8] Cisco, "Nuova Systems Acquisition Marks Another Major Step in Cisco's Data Center Efforts" (April 8, 2008), http://newsroom.cisco.com/dlls/2008/hd_040808b.html.

[9] Paul Venezia, "Review: Cisco's Unified Computing System Wows," *InfoWorld* (November 10, 2009), http://infoworld.com/d/hardware/test-center-reviewcisco-ucs-wows-603 (accessed November 19, 2009).

[10] Marthin de Beer, personal interview (January 21, 2009).

[11] Scott Anthony, "The Disruptors of the Decade," *Harvard Business Review* (January 14, 2010), http://blogs.hbr.org/anthony/2010/01/disruptors_of_the_decade_the_r.html (accessed January 28, 2010).

Chapter 3

[1] Neil Winton, "Manufacturers' Electric Dreams Likely to Stumble on Forecaster's Reality." *Detroit News* (July 31, 2009).

[2] Experian Hitwise, "Google Receives 71 Percent of Searches in September 2009," *Experian* (October 6, 2009), http://www.hitwise.com/us/press-center/press-releases/google-searches-sept-09 (accessed October 21, 2009).

[3] Apple, 2001, 10-K (Apple's annual SEC filing), http://phx.corporate-ir.net/phoenix.zhtml?c=107357&p=irol-SECText&TEXT=aHR0cDovL2NjYm4u MTBrd2l6YXJkLmNvbS94bWwvZmlsaW5nLnhtbD9yZXBvPXRlbmsmaXBhZ2 U9MTU2MjAwMyZhdHRhY2g9T04mc1hCUkw9MQ%3d%3d.

[4] "Apple Inc.—Finance," *Google*, http://www.google.com/finance?client=ob&q=NASDAQ:AAPL (accessed February 17, 2010).

[5] "ABI: Home Networking Market Slowing, Hits $74 Billion," *Consumer Electronics Daily News* (April 6, 2009), http://www.cedailynews.com/2009/04/abi-home-networking-market-slowing-hits-74-billion.html.

[6] "Zoinks! 20 Hours of Video Uploaded Every Minute!" *YouTube* (May 5, 2009), http://youtube-global.blogspot.com/2009/05/zoinks-20-hours-of-videouploaded-every_20.html.

[7] "Video Metrix—comScore, Inc." *ComScore, Inc.*, http://www.comscore.com/Press_Events/Press_Releases/2009/6/Americans_Viewed_a_Record_16.8_Billion_Videos_Online_in_April.

[8] WebEx, "Subaru achieves industry first with WebEx Training Center," 2006, http://static.webex.com/fileadmin/webex/documents/enterprise/pdf/manufacturing/casestudy_subaru.pdf.

9 "Gartner Says Worldwide Web Conference and Team Collaboration Software Market On Pace to Grow 22 Per Cent in 2008," *Gartner* (October 30, 2008), http://www.gartner.com/it/page.jsp?id=788813.

Chapter 4

1 Dan Gilmore, "Worst Supply Chain Disasters," *Supply Chain Digest* (January 26, 2006), http://www.scdigest.com/assets/FirstThoughts/06-01-26.cfm (accessed February 16, 2010).

2 "Escada," *Fashion Encyclopedia* (February 16, 2010), www.fashionencyclopedia.com/Da-Es/Escada.html.

3 Escada AG, "Fiscal Year 2002-2003 Annual Report," www.edob-abwicklung.de/gb_eng03/index.php?cont=cont/seite100.php.

4 "Escada AG," *Funding Universe* (February 16, 2010), www.fundinguniverse.com/company-histories/ESCADA-AG-Company-History.html.

5 Escada AG, "Fiscal Year 2007-2008 Annual Report," http://www.edob-abwicklung.de/gb_eng08/index.php?cont=cont/seite110.php.

6 Izzy Grinspan, "Poor Escada Sport in Soho Never Got a Chance to Shine," *Racked NY2* (February 6, 2010), http://ny.racked.com/archives/2010/02/03/poor_escada_sport_in_soho_never_got_a_chance_to_shine.php (accessed February 16, 2010).

7 Alia Rajput, "Escada Plans Expansion to Make Profit, End Insolvency," *Second City Style*, Web log post (January 28, 2010), http://secondcitystyle.typepad.com/second_city_style/2010/01/escada-plans-expansion-to-make-profit-end-insolvency-.html (accessed February 16, 2010).

8 Michael Kanellos, "Dell Grabs PC Top Spot from Compaq," *ZDNet* (April 20, 2001), http://news.zdnet.co.uk/hardware/0,1000000091,2085732,00.htm.

9 Abrahm Lustgarten, "Dell Beats Wal-Mart as 'Most Admired,'" *Fortune* (February 22, 2005), http://money.cnn.com/2005/02/21/news/fortune500/most_admired/.

10 Juan C. Perez and Grant Gross, "HP overtakes Dell in PC sales: IT giant regains lead of the worldwide market," *PC Advisor*, IDG (October 19, 2006), http://www.pcadvisor.co.uk/news/index.cfm?NewsID=7375.

11 Ben Rooney, "Dell's earnings slip despite rising sales," *CNN Money* (August 28, 2008), http://money.cnn.com/2008/08/28/news/companies/earns_dell/index.htm.

12 Dell, "2009 10-K," 5 and HP, "2008 Annual Report," 16.

13 Brian Caulfield, "Why Dell Isn't The Next Apple," *Forbes* (March 31, 2008), http://www.forbes.com/2008/03/31/dell-turnaround-research-tech-cx_bc_0331techdell.html.

14 "World's Most Admired Companies: Top 50." *Fortune* (March 16, 2009), http://money.cnn.com/magazines/fortune/mostadmired/2009/full_list/.

15 Larry Barrett, "Cisco's $2.25 billion mea culpa," *CNET* (May 9, 2001), http://news.cnet.com/2100-1033-257278.html.

Chapter 5

[1] Emily Maltby, "Chrysler Dealerships Fight Closings." *Wall Street Journal* (December 31, 2009), http://online.wsj.com/article/SB10001424052748704152804574628293363885148.html (accessed January 12, 2010).

[2] Christopher Scinta, Tiffany Kary, and Mike Ramsey, "Chrysler Asks Leave to Cancel 789 Dealer Agreements," *Bloomberg.com* (May 14, 2009), http://www.bloomberg.com/apps/news?sid=ayv7Vwsy1QRo&pid=20601087 (accessed January 2010).

[3] Jonathan Fahey, "The Lexus Nexus," *Forbes* (June 21, 2004), http://www.forbes.com/forbes/2004/0621/068.html (accessed January 12, 2010).

[4] Associated Press, "Amenities Enliven Auto Dealerships," *Washington Post* (December 12, 2007), http://www.washingtonpost.com/wp-dyn/content/article/2007/12/12/AR2007121200142_pf.html (accessed January 12, 2010).

[5] "Exceptional Service Satisfaction Enhances Dealer and Manufacturer Profitability Through Improved Customer Retention, Even as Vehicle Sales Decline," *J.D. Power and Associates*, posted February 25, 2009, http://www.jdpower.com/corporate/news/releases/pressrelease.aspx?ID=2009030 (accessed January 12, 2010).

[6] "Q2 2009 and Historical ACSI Scores," *American Customer Satisfaction Index*, http://www.theacsi.org/index.php?option=com_content&task=view&id=197&Itemid=206 (accessed January 13, 2010).

[7] As measured on a 5-point scale by Walker Information, a third-party hired to survey customers on Cisco's behalf.

[8] Jim Kavanaugh, telephone interview, March 5, 2009.

Chapter 6

[1] Regina Fazio Maruca, "The Right Way to Go Global: An Interview with Whirlpool CEO David Whitwam," *Harvard Business Review* (March-April 1994), http://hbr.org/1994/03/the-right-way-to-go-global-an-interview-with-whirlpool-ceo-david-whitwam/ar/1.

[2] Apala Chavan, Beena Prabhu, and Sarit Arora, "The Washing Machine That Ate My Sari—Mistakes in Cross-Cultural Design," *Interactions Magazine* XVI (2009): 1, http://interactions.acm.org/content/?p=1205 (accessed January–February 2009).

[3] Whirlpool Annual Report (1997).

[4] N. Bhan, "The World Washer; Whirlpool Enters the Indian Market," case study, Whirlpool Corporation (1990), http://www.emergingfutureslab.com/about.html.

[5] "How Did Nokia Succeed in the Indian Mobile Market, While Its Rivals Got Hung Up?" *India Knowledge@Wharton* (August 23, 2007), http://knowledge.wharton.upenn.edu/india/article.cfm?articleid=4220.

[6] James Ashton, "Nokia in search of a stronger signal," *Times Online* (February 14, 2010), http://business.timesonline.co.uk/tol/business/industry_sectors/technology/ article7026228.ece.

[7] Telecom Regulatory Authority of India, "Telecom Subscription data as on 31st December 2009," Press Release No. 8 (January 27, 2010), http://www.trai.gov.in/WriteReadData/trai/upload/PressReleases/721/Pr27jan2010no8.pdf.

[8] Jack Ewing, "How Nokia Users Drive Innovation," *BusinessWeek* (April 30, 2008).

[9] Gartner, "Gartner Says Worldwide Smartphone Sales Reached Its Lowest Growth Rate With 3.7 Per Cent Increase in Fourth Quarter of 2008," Gartner, Inc. (March 11, 2009), http://www.gartner.com/it/page.jsp?id=910112 (accessed January 15, 2010).

[10] Jeffrey R. Immelt, "Own The Future," Cisco Global Sales Meeting, Las Vegas, Nevada (Speech August 14, 2007).

[11] From "How GE Is Disrupting Itself" by Jeffrey R. Immelt, Vijay Govindarajan, and Chris Trimble, *Harvard Business Review*, October 2009. Excerpt reprinted with permission of *Harvard Business Review*.

[12] Media Eghbal, "Special Report: Developing world to overtake advanced economies in 2013," *Euromonitor* (February 19, 2009), http://www.euromonitor.com/Articles.aspx?folder=Special_Report_Developing_world_to_overtake_advanced_economies_in_2013&print=true.

[13] "Emerging Markets Infrastructure: Just Getting Started," Morgan Stanley (July 16, 2008), http://www.morganstanley.com/views/perspectives/articles/11203698-41a0-11de-a1b3-c771ef8db296.html.

[14] "The new champions: Emerging markets are producing examples of capitalism at its best," *The Economist* (September 18, 2008), http://www.economist.com/specialreports/displaystory.cfm?story_id=12080711&source=login_payBarrier.

[15] "How much proven crude oil reserves exist in the world?" Organization of the Petroleum Exporting Countries (OPEC), http://www.opec.org/opec_web/en/180.htm.

[16] Aaron Pava, "Who has the oil?" *Energy Bulletin*, Post Carbon Institute (November 17, 2007), http://www.energybulletin.net/node/37329.

[17] "Worldwide Look at Reserves and Production," *Oil and Gas Journal* 106 (December 22, 2008): 48, 22–23, http://www.naturalgas.org/Images/World%20Natural%20Gas%20Reserves.jpg.

[18] U.S. Geological Survey, Mineral Commodity Summaries (January 2007), http://minerals.usgs.gov/minerals/pubs/commodity/copper/coppemcs07.pdf.

[19] "Emerging Markets Infrastructure: Just Getting Started," Morgan Stanley (July 16, 2008), http://www.morganstanley.com/views/perspectives/articles/11203698-41a0-11de-a1b3-c771ef8db296.html.

[20] Population Division of the Department of Economic and Social Affairs of the United Nations Secretariat, "World Population Prospects: The 2006 Revision" and "World Urbanization Prospects: The 2007 Revision Population Database," http://esa.un.org/unup/index.asp?panel=2 (accessed February 19, 2010).

[21] Ibid.

[22] The Economist, ed., *The Economist Pocket World in Figures* 2008th ed. (London: The Economist Newspaper Limited, 2008), 22.

[23] "United Nations Human Settlements Programme 2008 Annual Report," Rep. no. 1050/08E, 1120th ed., Vol. HS. 2009, Print 09E.

[24] "India & Asia Operations: Success in India," *Appliance Magazine* (April 2003), http://www.appliancemagazine.com/editorial.php?article=168 (accessed January 14, 2010).

Chapter 7

[1] Nicole Perlroth, "Dean Kamen's Legacy Project," *Forbes* (August 24, 2009), http://www.forbes.com/forbes/2009/0824/thought-leaders-segwaydean-kamen-legacy-project.html (accessed October 9, 2009).

[2] Gary Rivlin, "Segway's Breakdown," *Wired* (March 2003), http://www.wired.com/wired/archive/11.03/segway.html (accessed October 9, 2009).

[3] Carlton Reid, "San Francisco bans Segways on sidewalks, bike paths," *The Register* (January 7, 2003), http://www.theregister.co.uk/2003/01/07/san_francisco_bans_segways/ (accessed October 9, 2009).

[4] The Segway Human Transporter, Frequently Asked Questions, http://www.segway.com/downloads/pdfs/Frequently_Asked_Questions_General.pdf.

[5] Perlroth, "Dean Kamen's Legacy Project."

[6] Alex Hutchinson, "Recycling Myths: PM Debunks 5 Half Truths about Recycling," *Popular Mechanics* (November 10, 2008), http://www.popularmechanics.com/science/earth/4290631.html?page=2 (accessed February 20, 2010).

[7] NextStep Recycling, "NextStep Recycling no longer accepting EPS foam for recycling," *PRLog* (June 27, 2009), http://www.prlog.org/10268692-nextstep-recycling-no-longer-accepting-eps-foam-for-recycling.html (accessed October 9, 2009).

[8] "Fortune 500 2009: Fortune 1000 1–100," *CNN Money*, http://money.cnn.com/magazines/fortune/fortune500/2009/full_list/ (accessed March 23, 2010).

[9] Cisco, "Cisco Systems Sets Guinness World Record with the World's Highest Capacity Internet Router," *Cisco.com*, http://newsroom.cisco.com/dlls/2004/prod_070104.html (accessed October 23, 2009).

[10] Rachael McBrearty and Brian Suckow, "The Economics of Collaboration at Cisco," (2009, pp. 1–4), *Cisco IBSG*, http://www.cisco.com/web/about/ac79/docs/pov/Economics_Collaboration_POV_FINAL_041009.pdf (accessed November 19, 2009).

[11] Rachael McBrearty and Joel Barbier, Cisco Internet Business Solutions Group, November 2009.

[12] "Collaboration: The Next Revolution in Productivity and Innovation," (2008, white paper), The Cisco Business Transformation Series: Collaboration, Cisco Systems, Inc.

[13] John Chambers, "Keynote," Cisco Live, San Francisco, California (speech given June 27, 2009).

14 "Byte Level Research Announces Best Global Web Sites of 2010," *Byte Level Research: Think Outside the Country* (March 4, 2010), http://www.bytelevel. com/news/reportcard2010.html (accessed March 23, 2010).

Chapter 8

1 ESPN Olympic Sports, "Anthony confident at Olympic team's first practice," *ESPN.com* (July 27, 2004), http://sports.espn.go.com/oly/summer04/basketball/ news/story?id=1846982 (accessed December 16, 2009).

2 ESPN Olympic Sports, "U.S.: 3-for-24 from 3-point range," *ESPN.com* (August 17, 2004), http://sports.espn.go.com/oly/summer04/basketball/news/story?id= 1859825 (accessed December 16, 2009).

3 Damon Hack, "Puerto Rico Upsets United States Men," *The New York Times* (August 15, 2004), http://www.nytimes.com/2004/08/15/sports/olympics/ 15CND-HOOPS.html (accessed December 16, 2009).

4 Experience Festival, "Garmin—Founders and Company Origins," *Global Oneness*, http://www.experiencefestival.com/a/Garmin_-_Founders_and_ Company_Origins/id/5074789 (accessed December 17, 2009).

5 Anya Kamenetz, "The World's 50 Most Innovative Companies," *Fast Company* (February 2010), http://www.fastcompany.com/mic/2010/industry/most- innovative-sports-companies (accessed February 20, 2010).

6 Mike Krzyzewski, "Mike Krzyzewski Interview: Collegiate Basketball Cham- pion," Academy of Achievement: Museum of Living History (May 22, 1997), http://www.achievement.org/autodoc/page/krz0int-1 (accessed December 16, 2009).

7 Matt Thomas, "Catching up with Carmelo Anthony," Team USA, United States Olympic Committee (May 28, 2009), http://basketball.teamusa.org/news/article/ 13137 (accessed December 21, 2009).

8 Mitch Lawrence, "It's commitment that takes medal for U.S. basketball," *NY Daily News* (August 25, 2008), http://www.nydailynews.com/sports/ 2008olympics/2008/08/24/2008-08-4_its_commitment_that_takes_medal_for_ us_b.html (accessed December 21, 2009).

Chapter 9

1 Gina Imperato, "Harley Shifts Gears," *Fast Company* (June 30, 1997), http:// www.fastcompany.com/magazine/09/harley.html (accessed January 7, 2010).

2 From "Harley's Leadership U-Turn" by Rich Teerlink, *Harvard Business Review*, July–August 2000. Excerpt reprinted with permission of *Harvard Busi- ness Review*.

3 Imperato, "Harley Shifts Gears."

4   Philip A. Chansler, Paul M. Swamidass, and Cortlandt Cammann, "Self-manag-
    ing work teams: An empirical study of group cohesiveness in 'natural work
    groups' at a Harley-Davidson Motor Company plant," *Small Group Research*
    Vol. 34, No.1 (February 2003): 1, 107.

5   Harley-Davidson, "Harley-Davidson Updates Guidance as Result of Strike,"
    (February 27, 2007), http://investor.harley-davidson.com/releasedetail.cfm?
    ReleaseID=231351 (accessed January 7, 2010); "Harley-Davidson Reports
    Fourth Quarter and Full Year Results For 2007," (February 27, 2007),
    http://investor.harley-davidson.com/releasedetail.cfm?ReleaseID=289615
    (accessed January 7, 2010).

6   Knowledge Editor, "Hog Futures Down," *Knowledge@Wharton* (July 9, 2009),
    http://knowledgetoday.wharton.upenn.edu/2009/07/hog-futures-down.html
    (accessed January 7, 2010).

7   Harley-Davidson, Inc., "Harley-Davidson, Inc. selects investment banking firm
    to assist in sale of MV Agusta," *Harley-Davidson* (November 19, 2009),
    http://www.harley-davidson.com/wcm/Content/Pages/HD_News/Company/
    newsarticle.jsp?locale=en_US&articleLink=News/0608_press_release.hdnews
    &newsYear=2009&history=archive (accessed January 7, 2010).

8   Bruce Caldwell, "Harley Shifts Into Higher Gear," *InformationWeek Online*
    (November 30, 1998), http://www.informationweek.com/711/11iuhar.htm;
    jsessionid=Q5IKBLUWDQJSLQE1GHPCKH4ATMY32JVN (accessed January
    7, 2010).

9   Randy Pond, personal interview (August 31, 2009).

10 Consumer Electronics Association, "Consumer Electronics to Grow in 2010,
    According to CEA Forecast" (January 7, 2010), http://www.ce.org/
    Press/CurrentNews/press_release_detail.asp?id=11861 (accessed January 9,
    2010).

11 "New Consumer Electronics and Informational Technologies" articles, *U.S.
    Consumer Electronics Industry Today* (June 14, 2005), http://www.nceita.org/us-
    consumer-electronics-industry-today.html (accessed January 9, 2010).

12 "YouTube—YouTube Fact Sheet," *YouTube*, http://www.youtube.com/t/
    fact_sheet (accessed October 25, 2009).

13 Jim Duffy, "Cisco will be hard pressed to match 2009," *Network World* (Decem-
    ber 17, 2009), http://www.networkworld.com/news/2009/121709-outlook-cisco.
    html (accessed December 24, 2009).

INDEX